silent witness 2ND EDITION REVISED

HOW FORENSIC ANTHROPOLOGY IS USED TO SOLVE THE WORLD'S TOUGHEST CRIMES

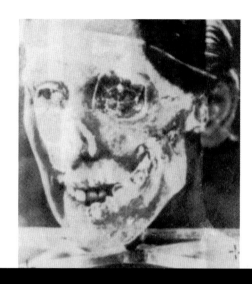

silent witness 2ND EDITION REVISED

HOW FORENSIC ANTHROPOLOGY IS USED TO SOLVE THE WORLD'S TOUGHEST CRIMES

ROXANA FERLLINI

FIREFLY BOOKS

A FIREFLY BOOK

Published by Firefly Books Ltd. 2012

First printing

Publisher Cataloging-in-Publications Data (U.S.)

Ferllini, Roxana.
    Silent witness : how forensic anthropology is used to
solve the world's toughest crimes / Roxana Ferllini.
2nd ed., rev.
[224] p. : ill. (some col.);   cm.
Includes bibliographical references and index.
ISBN-13: 978-1-77085-118-4 (pbk.)
1. Forensic anthropology. 2. Forensic sciences. 3. Criminal
investigation. I. Title.
364.125 dc23   RA1059.F4755 2012

Library and Archives Canada Cataloguing in Publication

Ferllini, Roxana
    Silent witness: how forensic anthropology is used
to solve the world's toughest crimes / Roxana Ferllini. —
2nd ed.
Includes bibliographical references and index.
ISBN 978-1-77085-118-4
    1. Forensic anthropology. 2. Forensic sciences.
3. Criminal investigation. I. Title.
GN69.8.F47 2012   363.25   C2012-901851-1

Published in the United States by
Firefly Books (U.S.) Inc.
PO Box 1338, Ellicott Station
Buffalo, New York 14205

Published in Canada by
Firefly Books Ltd.
66 Leek Crescent
Richmond Hill, Ontario L4B 1H1

Printed in China

This book was designed and produced by
Quintet Publishing Limited
6 Blundell Street London N7 9BH

For Quintet:

1st Edition
Project Editor: Corinne Masciocchi
Editor: Ian Penberthy
Art Directors: Simon Daley and Sharanjit Dhol
Designer: Roger Kohn
Creative Director: Richard Dewing
Publisher: Oliver Salzmann

2nd Edition
Project Editor: Julie Brook
Designer: Rod Teasdale
Art Director: Michael Charles
Picture Researchers: Sarah Bell and Jenny Faithfull
Editorial Director: Donna Gregory
Publisher: Mark Searle

Contents

Foreword

by Dr. Cyril Wecht, M.D., J.D.

Official governmental medicolegal investigation of violent and suspicious deaths is an essential component of the criminal justice system. The cause, manner, and mechanism of death must be determined by well-trained, competent forensic scientists in order for law enforcement and prosecutorial personnel to pursue their investigations in a logical and focused manner. And, of course, for the guilty person ultimately to be convicted and the innocent individual to be exonerated, it is necessary that modern day techniques be utilized by various kinds of forensic scientists. Included among these professional experts is the forensic anthropologist.

When skeletal fragments are found, the first step is to determine if they are human or animal. Once this has been established and the remains unearthed are skeletal, semi-skeletal, incomplete, fragmented, or too decomposed for identification by fingerprints, dentition, or recognition of facial features, an experienced forensic anthropologist must be called upon to assist in their identification.

By virtue of training in osteology and human growth, as well as forensic archeological experience in dealing with skeletal remains, the forensic anthropologist is uniquely prepared to deal with incomplete skeletons of individuals who may have died some time ago.

Forensic anthropologists also provide evidence and testimony in civil cases on such diverse topics as probability of relationship among members of families who have been separated, and motor vehicular accident/injury correlations, to name but a few. Additionally, they are called upon to assist in the examination of remains in air crashes that require the identification of badly burned and fragmented bodies for various personal and legal purposes. Such was the case in the United States where thousands of deaths were caused by the September 11, 2001 terrorist attacks.

Forensic anthropology and forensic pathology are two closely linked sciences and the expertise of one often complements that of the other allowing a definitive conclusion to be reached. It is sometimes necessary for the forensic pathologist to perform an autopsy without access to any clinical history or identity of the deceased. Consequently, the identification process, which may be difficult due to injuries or postmortem changes, is extremely important. This is where the skills and knowledge of the forensic anthropologist come into play and, working closely together, critical determinations can be reached.

The areas of interest and expertise of forensic pathologists and physical anthropologists overlap to some extent. This is true with regard to many other areas of forensic science that relate directly to the human body. However, the forensic pathologist, functioning as a coroner or medical examiner, should not be expected, nor should he or she be so intellectually arrogant as to assume ,to be so well versed in all these spheres as to not require input from other forensic specialists in determining the cause, manner, mechanism, and occasionally, the time and place of death, as well as establishing the identity of the decedent.

Roxana Ferllini, an experienced and acknowledged expert in the field of forensic anthropology, has written a comprehensive and compelling account of the various components of forensic anthropology and the ways in which experts in this fascinating field can provide invaluable services in the investigation and solution of homicides and other crimes. *Silent Witness* is backed up with a selection of well-chosen case studies that illustrate the complex and intriguing science that is forensic anthropology.

In August 1999, a severely decomposed and extensively skeletonized body was found buried in the ground of a farmhouse basement near Pittsburgh, when the current owners began to dig up a coal bin in anticipation of laying a concrete floor for a new furnace they planned to install. They were only about one foot deep when one of the shovels struck something in the dirt. What initially was thought to be a piece of wood turned out to be a leg bone with a man's shoe attached to it.

T he police were called, and promptly notified the local Coroner. The scene was documented via extensive written notes, photographic and video-graphic images, and archeological mapping. Tool marks were identified in the burial walls— the size and configuration of these suggested a rounded and pointed implement, such as a spade, had been used to dig the hole.

Forensic Analysis

The first step comprised an examination of the remains to ascertain if all the bones were present by laying them out to depict a complete skeletal representation. The skeleton was found to be complete and, after detailed laboratory analysis, various determinations and calculations were made: All the bones were examined based upon measurements of the long bones, examination of the skull and pelvic bones, and analysis of the epiphyseal lines (the end parts of the long bone). These differ tremendously between males and females. The skull and pelvic

bones assist in determining sex, and the long bones help to establish the age of an individual.

The analysis concluded that the victim was a 50-year-old Caucasoid male, 5 ft 8 in to 6 ft 3 in (173 cm to 190 cm) tall. Microscopic and radiological examinations were utilized to differentiate between antemortem and postmortem trauma. Also evident were stab wounds and gunshot trauma.

An autopsy examination was then conducted by a forensic pathologist. X-rays revealed numerous shotgun pellets in the left chest area. Two articles of clothing were submitted for analysis, one of which appeared to be an outer shirt, and the other a T-shirt-type garment. Both of these revealed multiple tears on the left side of the back. Some similar defects were also noted on

the right front side of both the outer and inner shirt garments. These tears were consistent with, and suggestive of, defects produced by multiple stab wounds to the chest.

Also present on both garments on the upper left-hand side was a fairly symmetrical, circular defect, surrounded by numerous, smaller holes. The large, circular configuration measured 2 in (5cm) in diameter when the garment was stretched. The surrounding small holes were consistent with, and strongly suggestive of, a shotgun pellet pattern.

The bones were identified and separated into component parts, i.e., skull, scapulae (shoulder blades), ribs, upper extremities, pelvic bones, lower extremities, vertebral column, hands, and feet. The skull showed no defects such as to suggest blunt force,

General view of excavation after the burial pit outline has been defined.

right Close-up view of the middle and upper torso of the body at autopsy following the removal of clothing (cranial direction to the right of the image). Note adipocere formation at mid torso and exposure of upper ribs.

penetrating, or perforating injuries. The sternum (breastbone) was intact, as were the vertebrae, with no evidence of blunt force, except for the posterior portions of two cervical vertebrae, which revealed fractures.

Some ribs demonstrated defects and fractures, including one which had completely fractured. These were considered to be consistent with injuries caused by stab wounds. Other ribs also showed several small defects but no complete fractures. These were more likely to have been caused by shotgun pellets.

The right tibia appeared to have a slightly increased curvature. This was consistent with the history of an old injury to the right leg (of the suspected individual), which reportedly caused him to walk with a noticeable limp.

Summary

A white male over the age of 50 years was excavated from a shallow grave in the basement of a farmhouse. The grave was 3¼ ft by 5 ft (99 cm by 152 cm) wide and about 3 ft (91 cm) deep. A rounded tool, such as a spade, was probably used to dig the grave. The individual was lying on his left side, legs bent at the hip and knees. The arms were extended in front of the body. The position of the shirt and pants suggested that the body had been dragged by the legs. Most of the body was devoid of soft tissue except for much of

the thorax, which presented a thick layer of adipocere, a waxlike fatty substance formed during decomposition.

Postmortem interval was difficult to establish, but it appeared to be longer than five years. Examination of the clothing was strongly suggestive of multiple stab wounds and one shotgun blast.

The bones revealed defects of two cervical vertebrae, consistent with recent antemortem traumatic injuries. There were also defects of several right ribs including fractures, which would be consistent with antemortem trauma. The left ribs showed minimal defects, which were suggestive of antemortem injury.

The skeleton presented evidence of several instances of perimortem trauma, including a shotgun blast to the left side of the neck/upper thorax. Sharp force trauma was noted in the form of a defect of the right scapula associated with a nick of one of the underlying ribs. The force of this blow fractured the scapula and three ribs. A second similar defect close to the first is also noted. A sharp implement was indicated, although it was not possible to identify a specific

weapon. DNA analysis was performed to corroborate the identity of the deceased.

As a result of these forensic scientific findings, the deceased's wife and stepdaughter confessed to having stabbed the victim several times in the bedroom, following a heated domestic argument. Then, as he appeared to still be alive, one of them fired a shotgun at his chest while he lay on the floor. They then carried the body downstairs and buried it in the basement of their farmhouse, where they continued to live for another nine months. The couple who discovered the body had lived there for 13 years before the remains were uncovered.

The stepdaughter ultimately pled guilty and testified against her mother, who was convicted of first-degree murder in a jury trial.

This case illustrates how forensic anthropologists and forensic pathologists collaborate to establish the identity of the deceased; determine the cause, mechanism, and manner of death; and provide the necessary scientific testimony required by the criminal justice system to successfully prosecute a murder case.

1 Forensic Anthropology and Other Sciences

The skills of forensic anthropologists are required in a myriad of situations in which human remains need to be identified. A person's death can be precipitated by a variety of reasons—aviation disasters, explosions, fires, drowning, homicides, and violations of human rights. Ascertaining a victim's identity isn't always straightforward, especially when their remains are altered beyond recognition. This is where the knowledge of forensic anthropologists comes into play.

« In most instances, a body will have eggs deposited on it by flies. These eggs hatch rapidly into larvae, and their stage of development provides the forensic entomologist with an accurate time of death. »

Anthropology studies humankind, and divides into three key categories: archeology, cultural anthropology, and physical anthropology, also known as biological anthropology. The latter incorporates such subjects as human evolution, modern human variability, development and growth, genetics, human osteology (the study of bones), primatology (the study of monkeys and apes), and related subjects. Expertise in human osteology led to the involvement of physical anthropologists in forensics, the field that pertains directly to legal issues, popularly referred to as forensic anthropology.

Within modern forensics, forensic anthropology is an invaluable investigative tool for solving difficult and sensitive criminal cases, aiding the accurate identification of human remains of missing persons, accident victims, or those who suffered a far more traumatic and sinister fate at the hands of criminals.

Specifically, forensic anthropology identifies skeletal human remains where bones are the only evidence. Often, these may have been burned beyond recognition, or may have been mutilated by explosives, as the result of an airplane crash or train collision, for example. Forensic anthropologists often assist in the investigation of crime, such as a murder involving dismemberment of the victim, and frequently examine and analyze human remains that may be in a state of advanced decomposition. The skills of the forensic anthropologist are crucial in the recovery of individuals from crime scenes, whether buried or

right An exhumation of human remains being carried out under the watchful eyes of the police.

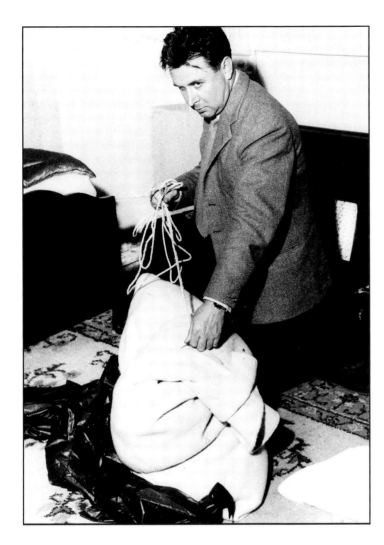

left Donald Hume, who murdered a man and disposed of the body, showing how he removed the remains from the apartment.

scattered on the surface, or in the case of human rights, in the opening of mass graves. In the latter case, its application ensures that the remains are attributed accurately to the individuals during their exhumation. The forensic anthropologist may also reconstruct remains, including skulls and other parts of the skeleton, to analyze the physical effects of traumas to the body, such as gunshot or other fatal wounds. Finally, the forensic anthropologist may be called upon when human remains cannot be identified by conventional means, for example facial characteristics or fingerprints, and produce a biological identification—sex, age, ancestry, stature, and individual traits.

Because of their expertise in identifying human remains, forensic anthropologists are instrumental in the investigation and management of crime scenes. By applying a variety of careful and precise archeological techniques, they can assist in the recovery of the victims. These techniques resemble those utilized in digs at archeological sites, where the remains of earlier civilizations are recovered, although slight variations may be necessary to meet legal requirements. The application of such techniques to a legal investigation is referred to as forensic archeology. The forensic anthropologist's role is to work alongside a team of other forensic investigators, each of whom collects and analyzes different types of evidence and data. These combined results

above A late 18th-century anatomy theater used to conduct anatomical demonstrations.

above right Medical students in the late 1800s, carrying out a dissection of a corpse.

help to form a complete picture of events. The findings may then be utilized during criminal trials and coroners' investigations, where the forensic anthropologist may be asked to give expert testimony.

The advent of forensic anthropology

Compared to other criminal sciences, forensic anthropology is a relatively new discipline. Its beginnings date back to the end of the 19th century and the studies conducted by Dr. Thomas Dwight (1843–1911). Based at Harvard University, Massachusetts, Dr. Dwight is referred to as the "Father of American Forensic Anthropology." Indeed, the origin, development, and refinement of this fascinating science occurred predominantly in the United States.

Dr. Dwight's analysis of human skeletons took place where the Harvard Medical School stands today, thanks to the donation of the land by Dr. Parkman (see case study No. 1). Being by profession an anatomist, Dwight was one of the first academics to take a particular interest in the clues that bones provide to a person's identity. It was soon realized that this information could be applied directly to the medicolegal field.

Dr. Dwight's research on bones, completed in a proper and thorough fashion for the first time, demonstrated how much the skeleton can tell us about an individual (see Chapter 2). Additionally, the variability between skeletons was analyzed in depth. Subjects covered included human stature and the statistical study of bones to determine sex, height, and age. The nature of Dwight's work made him a pioneer in the field, and sowed the seeds for the development and evolution of forensic anthropology.

Other leading forensic anthropologists

Dwight's pioneering work influenced others, who continued the research to assist forensic investigators in their task of identifying human remains solely by examining bones and determining their biological profile (biological identification).

Among Dr. Dwight's followers was Dr. George A. Dorsey (1869–1931). He studied anthropology at Harvard, and became involved in the sensational Luetgert case in Chicago (see case study No. 2).

During the first half of the 20th century, skeletal analysis became more established until, eventually, the Federal Bureau of Investigation (FBI) became interested in employing forensic anthropological analysis as an investigative tool in many of their cases. They called upon the services of anthropologists, including Dr. T. D. Stewart, an affiliate of the Smithsonian Institution. Dr. Stewart also helped identify casualties from World War II and the Korean War. When considering the effects of combat upon the human body, one must keep in mind that the weapons utilized have become progressively more devastating and capable of inflicting substantial wounds, making identification of individuals far more difficult and time-consuming.

The need to recover and identify deceased soldiers so that they could be repatriated and returned to their families became of paramount importance. Such work was carried out in World War II, in both the European and Pacific theaters of war.

above U.S. troops engaged in combat during the Korean War.

right Dr. T. D. Stewart at work.

right Live maggots grown in bottles for future analysis.

In 1976, the Central Identification Laboratory in Hawaii (CILHI) was established by the US government, today known as Joint POWMIA Accounting Command (Joint Prisoners of War Missing in Action Accounting Command). It still remains active, devoted to the identification and repatriation of American soldiers from World Wars I and II, the Korean War, and also the Vietnam conflict. Over the years, it has employed a great number of forensic scientists, including many forensic anthropologists.

These scientists travel to a variety of field locations, including the South Pacific, where they are required to recover and identify the remains of missing US service personnel. Preliminary analysis takes place in the country where the remains are discovered, with the participation of local forensic scientists. During this initial study, it is important to determine that the remains are not from the native population. This is accomplished by reference to the statistical characteristics that different populations exhibit at skeletal level. The remains are then taken to the laboratory in Hawaii and the final identification process initiated—a biological profile of each set of remains is created and compared to the available database. At the time of writing, it is estimated that tens of thousands of American soldiers are still officially "missing in action."

As a discipline, forensic anthropology became consolidated in 1972, when the Physical Anthropology Section was accepted at the American Academy of Forensic Science. Today, forensic anthropology is widely used to solve a variety of crimes, in particular genocide (see Chapter 8). International teams of forensic experts are regularly assembled by organizations such as the United Nations, to aid the identification and recovery of human remains throughout the world. Such efforts have involved the Argentine Forensic Anthropology Team, the Guatemalan Forensic Anthropology Foundation, and the Physicians for Human Rights in Boston, Massachusetts, among others.

A multidisciplinary approach

In a legal investigation, the forensic anthropologist works alongside several other investigators in the field.

The forensic pathologist analyzes soft tissue for any marks left on a body. Soft tissue may exhibit evidence of foul play, struggle, torture, or other physical traumas. A forensic pathologist is responsible for determining the cause and manner of death by carrying out an autopsy upon the remains.

Another scientific discipline related to forensic anthropology cases is forensic entomology. In most instances, a body will have eggs deposited on it by flies, which often occurs immediately after death. These eggs hatch rapidly into larvae, and their stage of development provides the forensic entomologist with an accurate time of death, vital information in a legal investigation. The species of larvae present upon the body indicate the time of year when the death took place, in addition to the climatic conditions at the time. Since the fly larvae consume the flesh of the remains, they also absorb any drugs, legal or illegal, that the deceased person may have ingested. Even if the remains are practically

below The Japanese tsunami in 2011 caused thousands of deaths. The identification of the victims can require a multidisciplinary approach. Here, rescue workers offer a prayer for a victim discovered in the rubble.

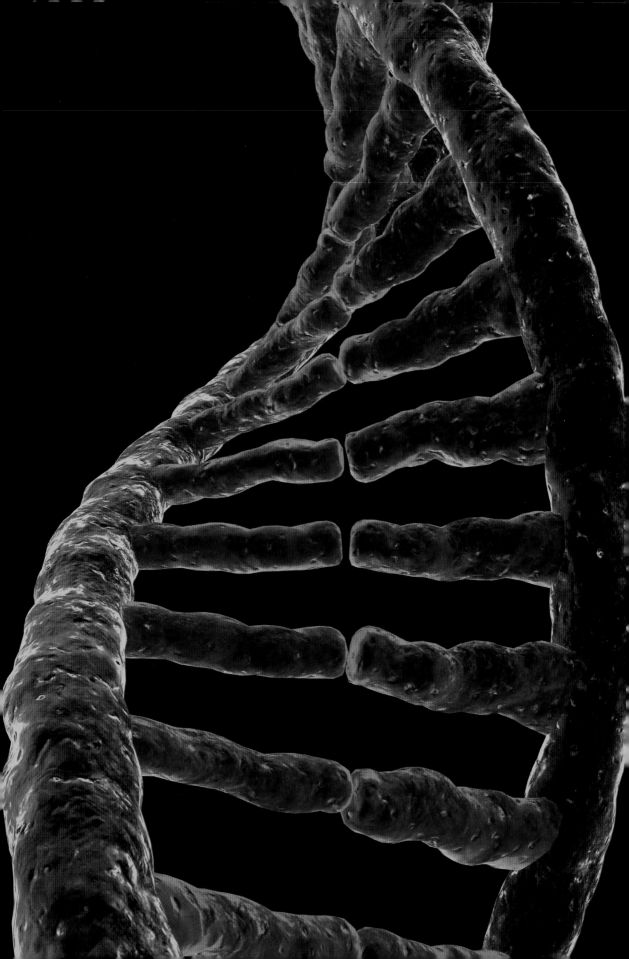

skeletonized, the larvae may still provide an accurate indication of any drugs present in the body at the time of death.

Forensic botanists also play an important role in criminal cases, since occasionally botanical matter (vegetation) is associated with the remains or the site being investigated, and the plants must therefore be identified. Forensic botanists can deduce if a body has been moved from its original resting place and, if so, can suggest the type of area from which it may have come. Additionally, they can link any plant matter from the scene with that found upon the victim's personal effects, or in his or her car or home. This is possible because plants can be identified through microscopic characteristics, such as seeds and spores. Also, many plants grow exclusively in particular areas and, often, localized ecosystems.

Some biologists specialize in molecular biology and can carry out DNA (deoxyribonucleic acid) analysis of the protein that carries a person's genetic blueprint. Although DNA is a positive means of identifying a body, the cooperation of a forensic anthropologist is often required, particularly if the remains of an individual are mixed with others, as in a mass grave. In such a situation, the remains require proper separation to determine how many bodies are present. If this is not done with care, it may be impossible to determine the biological profile of each individual. This information is essential, since each profile will be compared to a database of missing persons. The relatives of likely individuals from the database may then be contacted, and a DNA comparison carried out. This may lead to the case being resolved.

Forensic odontologists (dentists) also play a key role in the process of identifying the deceased, by analyzing the dental work upon the teeth present at the time of death. They then compare their analysis with an antemortem record. Dentures may also be used in this particular type of analysis. Anthropologists and odontologists are expected to work together when the remains of more than one person have become mixed, even in cases where the dental remains can be analyzed and compared with antemortem records.

Due to the multidisciplinary approach to forensic work, the investigation of criminal cases today involves far more comprehensive analysis than even a few decades ago, and produces more accurate results.

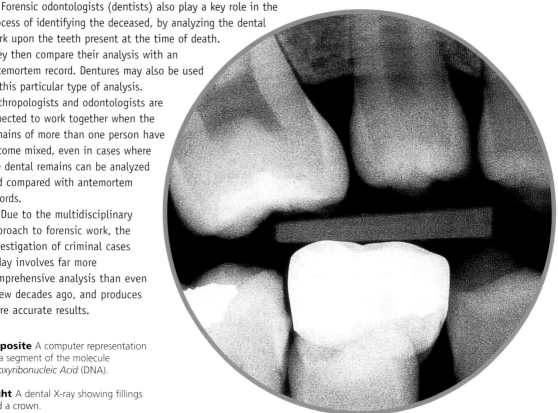

opposite A computer representation of a segment of the molecule *Deoxyribonucleic Acid* (DNA).

right A dental X-ray showing fillings and a crown.

Dr. John Webster

On Friday, November 23, 1849, 59-year-old Dr. George Parkman, a wealthy physician and prominent member of Boston society, disappeared.

Although a medical doctor by profession, most of Parkman's business dealings revolved around his extensive real-estate holdings and money lending. He would regularly collect what was owed to him in person, and usually on foot.

When last seen in public, he had been on his way to the Harvard Medical College to meet his friend and colleague, Dr. John W. Webster, a professor of chemistry and mineralogy.

Through his efforts, Dr. Webster attained a high social standing, but he was not very adept at managing his finances. To ease his financial burden, he decided to borrow money from Dr. Parkman. By 1849, he was in debt to Parkman to the tune of $2,432—a considerable sum for the time. To secure the loan, Webster mortgaged a variety of personal possessions, including a valuable mineral collection. To Dr. Parkman's great annoyance, he learned that Dr. Webster had arranged to offer the very same mineral collection for private sale, threatening the security placed on his loan to Dr. Parkman. With feelings of considerable anxiety, he decided to meet with Webster to clarify the matter.

TRIAL

OF

PROFESSOR JOHN W. WEBSTER

FOR THE

MURDER

OF

DOCTOR GEORGE PARKMAN.

REPORTED EXCLUSIVELY FOR THE N. Y. DAILY GLOBE.

PROFESSOR WEBSTER.

NEW YORK:

STRINGER & TOWNSEND, 222 BROADWAY.

PRINTED AT THE GLOBE OFFICE.

left Publication of the trial of Dr. Webster for the murder of Dr. George Parkman.

opposite above A drawing of Dr. Parkman as last seen before his murder.

opposite below A drawing illustrating the murder of Dr. Parkman in 1849.

For a week, no one knew of Dr. Parkman's whereabouts. A $3,000 reward was offered for information that would lead to his discovery. Then, with Christmas approaching, the janitor of the medical college, Ephraim Littlefield, raised the alarm. Suspicious of Webster, Littlefield visited his laboratory.

As he examined a stone wall in the laboratory, he made a shocking discovery—putrefying human remains had been concealed beneath a latrine. Eventually a human thorax was recovered, together with a set of false teeth and several pieces of burned bone.

Dr. Webster was arrested and put on trial at the beginning of 1850. This is considered by many to be the first truly sensational trial in America, and it gained the attention of thousands of Bostonians, large numbers of whom would gather outside the courthouse in the hope of witnessing the proceedings first hand. The trial also attracted close media coverage, including the attention of foreign journalists.

The police called upon the assistance of physicians and dentists to aid in the identification of the recovered remains. Among them was Dr. Oliver Wendell Holmes, an anatomist. The results of the analysis indicated that the remains were compatible with Dr. Parkman's description, closely matching his age, height, and build. Dr. Webster was found guilty of Parkman's murder and was sentenced to hang.

Today, more than 150 years after the murder, many question the validity of the trial's outcome. In particular, the "expert" testimony of Dr. Wendell Holmes is regarded with considerable caution. This is because, at the time, the necessary statistical knowledge of the human skeleton required to make an accurate estimate of the age, sex, and individual characteristics of skeletal remains had not been developed sufficiently.

Dr. Parkman donated the land upon which the Harvard Medical School stands. Ironically, it was here that Dr. Dwight, known as the "Father of American Forensic Anthropology," would carry out his research on the human skeleton.

Adolph Louis Luetgert

Originally a native of Germany, Adolph Louis Luetgert moved to the United States, where his line of work was meat processing. Realizing that his skills had wider potential, he decided to set up his own business, the A. L. Sausage & Packing Company, located on Diversey and Hermitage Avenue in the Lakeview area of Chicago.

In the 1880s, Luetgert married Louisa, a small and attractive woman many years younger than him. However, Luetgert's relationship with his young wife was often strained, and rumors persisted that he abused her physically, and that he regularly engaged in extramarital affairs.

During the spring of 1897, Luetgert was seen taking a stroll with his wife. This was the last time that Louisa was spotted alive. When her family became aware of her disappearance, they made urgent inquiries as to her whereabouts, but to no avail. As for Luetgert, he claimed that she had decided to leave him.

The police carried out an extensive search for the missing woman, interviewing people from the immediate area. Eventually, they took their search to Luetgert's sausage factory and, once there, several employees directed them to a large steam vat used for dipping sausages. What made the vat so notable was that unpleasant odors came from it, as well as an unidentifiable liquid. After close inspection, small pieces of bone were discovered in the vat, together with two gold earrings, one of which was inscribed with the initials "L.L."

These had been Louisa's wedding gift from her husband. As the search within the sausage factory widened, small pieces of burned bone were discovered near the vat, as were the remains of a burned corset and a tooth fragment.

These finds were sufficient for the police to arrest and jail Luetgert. He was accused of murdering and boiling his wife.

The trial began during the summer of the same year. Anthropologist Dr. George Dorsey and some of his colleagues from the Field Museum in Chicago, were called upon to analyze skeletal remains, including fragments from a leg, an arm, a hand, and a foot.

According to the testimony of Dr. Dorsey, the remains were human and belonged to a female. Other witnesses indicated that prior to Louisa's disappearance, Luetgert had purchased several hundred pounds of crude potash and had added it gradually to the vat where her remains were discovered. In his defense, Luetgert said that the potash was used to make soap, which he needed to clean the factory.

Luetgert was tried twice—the first trial produced a hung jury, but the second trial found him guilty, and he was sent to prison for life. He was incarcerated at Joliet State Penitentiary, where he died some years later, proclaiming his innocence throughout. This legal case can be said to be the first in which an anthropologist was called to testify as an expert witness.

opposite above Adolph and Louisa Luetgert.

opposite below Inside Luetgert's sausage factory, where Louisa's remains where discovered in a steam vat used for dipping sausages.

above The A. L. Sausage & Packing Company, Chicago.

Eugene Aram

The 18th-century case of Eugene Aram illustrates well the necessity of forensic anthropology as a tool for solving crimes. This particular case would have benefited greatly from the expertise required to correctly identify skeletal remains to bring about a sure conviction.

below Eugene Aram.

Aram had received a formal education, enabling him to open his own school. However, despite his education and the wide knowledge that he managed to accrue, the riches that he longed for were never close at hand.

To improve his financial situation and provide some extra income, Aram hit upon the idea of engaging in some theft on the side. He also decided to recruit others to his scheme, one of whom was Daniel Clarke.

Clarke had married into a wealthy family, and Aram suggested that he should order some goods from London, including some very expensive silver plate and jewelry, so that he might boost his visible wealth.

After the goods had been delivered, they disappeared, along with Clarke, never to be seen again. Because he had not yet paid for the items, many believed that Clarke had taken them

himself. However, in the meantime, he had agreed to meet Aram and another friend, Richard Houseman, outside St. Robert's Cave in Netherdale, Yorkshire. There, according to Houseman, Aram beat Clarke to death.

Thirteen years later, a laborer was digging for stone in Thistlehill, near Knaresborough, and unearthed some bones. The local consensus was that the remains probably belonged to Clarke. In due course, Aram's wife turned him in to the authorities, voicing her belief that her husband had killed Clarke, and that Houseman had been involved. Eventually Houseman was questioned, but his statements indicated that the bones could not belong to Clarke, since he had been buried exactly where he had been murdered, at St. Robert's Cave. Houseman provided a clear description of the area where the skeletal remains could be found, together with details of

the position in which the body had been laid to rest. Human remains were indeed recovered from the site he had identified during questioning, and Aram was duly arrested as a suspect in Clarke's murder. Although the authorities did not know with certainty that the bones discovered at the cave belonged to Clarke, Aram was detained at York Castle and charged with murder. His trial began during the summer of 1759 and he was shortly found guilty and sentenced to death. He was executed at York and his body hung in chains at Knaresborough.

The Aram case might have had a totally different outcome had a forensic anthropologist been able to produce an accurate analysis of the remains in question. Aram's own defense had centered upon the fact that there was no conclusive proof that the bones belonged to Clarke, but the court disagreed.

left A drawing re-enacting the murder of Daniel Clarke in 1745.

2 Bones Do Talk

Human bones are seen as a reflection of our inevitable death. Illustrations of bones form part of familiar images pointing to death or danger, as on pirate flags and poison bottles. When recovered from burial sites and examined by a trained eye, bones convey a variety of rich and fascinating stories about their history.

From a forensic perspective, bones provide information that allows them to be identified as belonging to a particular individual, offering us tantalizing clues as to how a person met their fate. Bones can also reveal the identity of a person, thereby solving many cases that would otherwise have gone unsolved.

The human body

The body of an adult human contains a total of 206 bones, which vary in size, thickness, and shape. Among the biggest of our bones is the femur (the thighbone), while the three ossicles that are to be found inside each of our ears are among the tiniest. Because bone is composed of dense minerals, mainly calcium, the skeleton can survive for many centuries after death. In time, buried bones may become fossilized as a result of mineralization after losing their true organic components. Fossilized bones have survived for millions of years, providing materials that may be utilized by paleontologists to reconstruct the past.

It is their capacity to survive the ravages of time and the elements that makes bones an ideal material in the identification of human remains by forensic means. Even after suffering the effects of fire, being raised from an underwater grave, or enduring attack by corrosive materials, bones have an uncanny knack of holding important clues as to the fate of the individuals to whom they belonged.

Teeth are constructed of hard and durable materials too, known as dentin, enamel, and cementum. These enable teeth to survive even better than bones, even when extreme methods are used in an attempt to conceal the identity of an individual. In some cases, where acids or other corrosive substances have been used to deface them, teeth may be altered by the process of decalcification, but they still remain to provide clues to the identity of the person concerned. Under this type of circumstance, dentures have also been rescued.

Human or not?

When provided with a set of bones to identify, there may be occasions when an anthropologist will conclude that some of them are not of human origin, particularly if the remains have been recovered from a rural area. It is rare for a complete animal skeleton to be presented for forensic analysis in the mistaken belief that it is human. However, in the case of an isolated bone, or small bone fragments, confusion may result if untrained eyes are involved in the recovery. Within the boundaries of the forensic sciences, however, assumptions are never made. Every artifact that is recovered is scrutinized carefully to determine its validity as evidence, as well as confirm that the bones are indeed human. Further examination of the samples will indicate whether the remains of more than one individual have been discovered.

« It is their capacity to survive the ravages of time that makes bones an ideal element in the identification of human remains by forensic means. Bones have an uncanny knack of holding important clues as to the fate of the individuals to whom they belonged. »

A forensic anthropologist's first task is to assemble the bones in anatomical order. This allows an assessment of the completeness of the skeleton, and will indicate if more than one individual has been recovered. If, after careful analysis, the remains of more than one individual are present, it is possible that a multiple murder may have been committed. It is through this careful and methodical process that animal bones would be recognized and set aside.

Experts can deduce whether a bone is human or not by the characteristics of its morphology, that is, the shape and character it displays. Such visible differences are due to the physical stresses and requirements that the bones of an animal are designed to meet, and also the manner of its locomotion. These individual characteristics develop over countless years through a process of gradual evolution. For example, the human skeleton possesses seven cervical vertebrae, which form the upper part of the vertebral spine and assist in supporting the skull. Giraffes also have seven cervical vertebrae, but their shape is very different to those of humans. This is because the giraffe's cervical vertebrae have developed to allow it to perform a specific task—browsing on the high vegetation of trees. Although this example may appear to be extreme, such differences are used by forensic anthropologists to eliminate items that are unrelated to the case concerned.

In North America, isolated bones from the paws of bears are discovered occasionally. These bones resemble those found in human hands and, as a result, police departments are contacted in the belief that the bones are the remains of people who have met their end through foul play. Once analyzed by a forensic anthropologist, however, any confusion is quickly cleared up.

Although differentiating human bones from those of animals may not be difficult, investigators who work in the field of osteology (the study of bone) may meet with great challenges. Great care must be exercised when dealing with fragments of immature skeletal remains of animals such as gorillas, horses, and sheep, as their morphologies in the early stages of development are similar to those of a human baby.

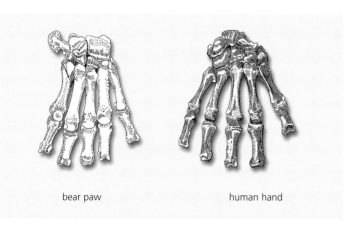

bear paw   human hand

above A giraffe has seven cervical vertebrae just as humans do.

left The anatomy of a bear paw closely resembles that of a human hand, thus possibly causing confusion.

Determining whether a set of teeth is human or not is much more straightforward than identifying fragmented bone remains. The form and characteristics of human dentition are distinctive. This is because, for the most part, humans consume soft or processed foods that do not require substantial chewing or tearing. Nonetheless, the top surfaces of teeth such as molars belonging to humans who regularly consume grains that are processed under grindstones, will wear down far more rapidly than those of populations where the processing of grains is different. The same may be said for groups that follow a traditional lifestyle in the northern latitudes, such as the Inuit, who from time to time use their teeth as an additional tool.

Biological profile

Compiling a biological profile is the next task that must be completed by a forensic anthropologist to assist in the identification of an individual. The eventual objective is to produce a positive identification for the police and legal teams so that they may investigate the death fully. A death certificate may also be completed upon the successful identification of the remains. In most Western and some non-Western societies, a death certificate is required by law, no matter what the manner of death. The certificate allows surviving relatives to collect insurance benefits, settle wills, and sell properties; it also permits surviving spouses to marry again if they wish.

The biological identification is accomplished by conducting a detailed study of skeletal and dental remains. In the case of a badly decomposed body, soft tissues such as skin and muscle must be removed with great care to avoid damaging the bones. In fact, accidental alterations to the bones during the removal of soft tissues may cause confusion, thereby hindering the investigation. Compiling the biological profile entails determining the sex, age, ancestry, stature, and any other notable characteristics of the person concerned; the results produce a presumptive profile, which then enables a move forward to a positive identification.

Sex

To determine the sex of an adult human skeleton, anthropologists look for physical landmarks that act as key indicators. There are many to be

SKELETAL DIFFERENCES BETWEEN MALES AND FEMALES

MALE	FEMALE
Bigger and heavier frame	Smaller and lighter frame
Prominent muscle insertions	Less obvious muscle insertions
Prominent and robust cranial features	Finer and lighter cranial features
Inclined frontal bone	Rounded frontal bone
Noticeable supraorbital ridge	Indiscernible supraorbital ridge
Top margin of the eye orbits is smooth to the touch	Top margin of the eye orbits is sharp to the touch
U-shaped palate	Parabolic-shaped palate
Square chin	Pointed chin
Flared jaw line	Parallel jaw line
Posterior part of skull has a noticeable protuberance	Posterior part of skull is smoother
Narrow pelvic bone	Flared pelvic bone to accommodate childbearing

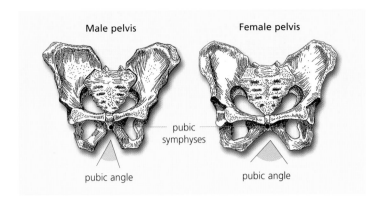

Male pelvis

Female pelvis

pubic symphyses

pubic angle

pubic angle

left The female pelvis has a wider subpubic angle to accommodate childbirth.

found in the 206 bones available, but some are more preferable than others. One of the main methods of establishing the sex of an individual is to rely on a phenomenon known as sexual dimorphism, which refers to the structural or physical differences between a male and female within any species. For example, in butterflies, some females are larger and display different colors than males of the same species. Conversely, in birds, males tend to be bigger than females and possess brighter-colored plumage. In humans, the main differences lie in the robustness of the male, who tends to have more muscle mass, with a resultant potential of greater bone size and physical strength than the female, whose bones are usually smaller.

Additionally, since female humans are predisposed to pregnancy and childbirth, their pelvic bones are shaped differently. Women's hipbones tend to flare out, permitting a larger space to accommodate the developing fetus. Moreover, the lower part of the pelvic girdle, which is formed by the left and right pubic bones, is wider, as it is through this space that part of the birthing process takes place.

Characteristics of the skull, including those of the mandible, can also be of help. Generally, the skull of a male human contains more prominent and robust features than that of a female. One particular

below left The male skull is characterized by a square chin and noticeable brow ridges.

below right The female skull is less robust and the chin is more pointed.

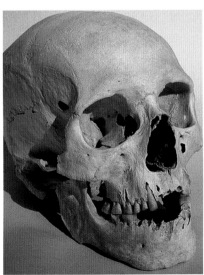

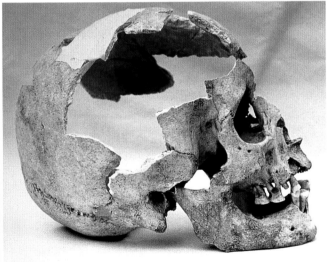

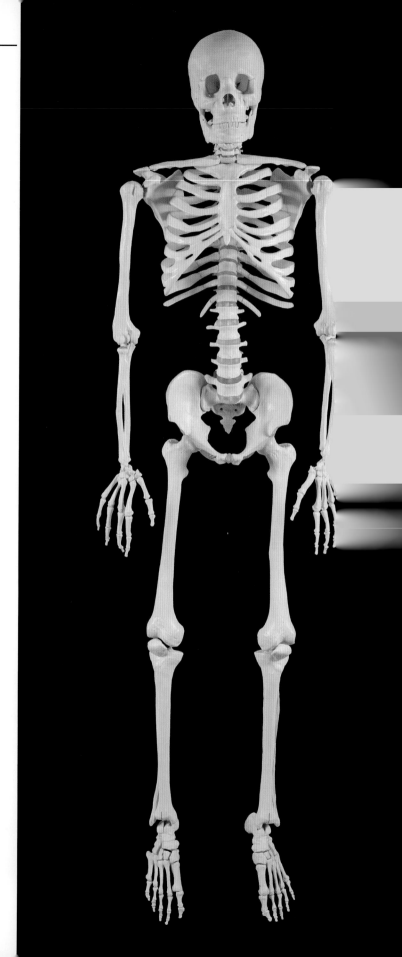

right The adult human skeleton has 206 bones of various shapes and sizes.

landmark is the supraorbital ridge, a bony protrusion just above the point where the eyebrows lie, which is very noticeable in males, but practically absent in females. Additionally, in the case of females, the forehead tends to be rounded, while in males it is inclined. Males also possess squarer chins, whereas the female chin is usually pointed.

Although the pelvis and the skull are the main indicators for sexing a body, measurements of other bones, such as those of the hands, may also be used to establish the gender of an individual. This might be the case when the pelvis or skull is absent, or in situations where the remains are severely fragmented or sparse.

In cases involving fetuses and children, an analysis may be difficult to conduct because of the developing stage of the skeleton. However, a trained forensic anthropologist may still be able to obtain results through a thorough and meticulous examination.

Age

Once the sex has been established, the age of the individual at death must be determined. Ascertaining the sex first is crucial, since in adult women the aging process at bone level progresses much more rapidly than in men. In some cases, osteoporosis may be present, altering the bone condition. Osteoporosis may result from menopause, so the sex of the individual is an important consideration before attempting to estimate age. Here, too, the anthropologist must look for key physical landmarks.

Infants, children, and teenagers experience a continual growth process, producing many landmarks throughout the skeleton and the dentition. The dental remains are particularly useful, because the teeth are still in the process of development. Children possess only 20 teeth, lacking premolars and the third molars, commonly known as the wisdom teeth. These initial, or deciduous, teeth are replaced eventually by a set of permanent teeth. This process of gradual dental development and maturation can be used to make an accurate assessment of the age of an individual.

The maturing process is noticeable in the bones too, since those of young individuals will not be developed fully or ossified (hardened). To allow the growth process to be completed, the bones are separated into

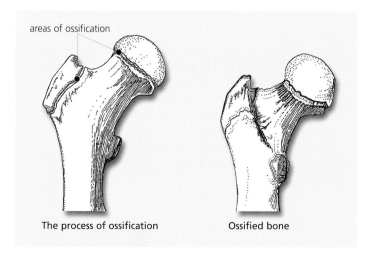

areas of ossification

The process of ossification   Ossified bone

left The top part of the femur (thigh bone) during the ossification process. Once the process is complete, the bone merges into one single bone.

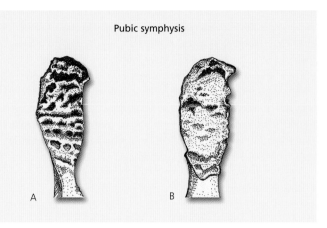

Pubic symphysis

A   B

above Thoracic vertebrae showing bony growths and bone degeneration.

several elements, which do not unify until maturity, when they form a single bone. This is very noticeable in the case of the longer bones, such as those of the arms and legs. The wrist bones also develop and change continually throughout childhood and early adolescence. When examining the remains of a fetus, the anthropologist may attempt an estimation of the age by measuring the length of the bones, indicating the time that has elapsed since conception.

In adults, the teeth will not help in the determination of age at death, since by the age of 20, the permanent dentition of 32 teeth will have ceased developing. Instead, the process of aging and degeneration of the bones is observed, and the most reliable landmark in the skeleton is the pubic symphysis—the point where the two pubic bones meet in the pelvic girdle. This particular area of the body undergoes a metamorphic change beginning at around the age of 18 and continuing throughout the life of the individual. The changes are uniform in males and females regardless of ancestry, making it the most common factor utilized in assessing age at the time of death.

As humans age, the bones tend to "wear out," and these visible alterations in the body also help to indicate age. For example, after the age of 35, small bony growths can occur in the vertebral spine, and the margins of each vertebra may become distorted.

Ancestry

These days, the word "race" can have negative connotations, so the terms "ancestry" or "biological affinity" are used instead. At the bone and dental level, three distinctions can be made: African or black descent; Caucasoid or white descent; and Mongoloid descent, which includes Native Americans, Inuit, and people of Asian descent. Although knowledge of ancestry is desirable in forensic cases, in practice it may be quite difficult to prove due to the wide human variability present in some populations. Additionally, different ancestries may present a mixture of characteristics within each affinity. Further complication occurs in the case of immature individuals, since their bones may still be forming and will not display the typical features present in adults.

For humans of African descent, the most obvious differences occur in the skull, which lacks a nasal spine and has the widest nasal aperture of any

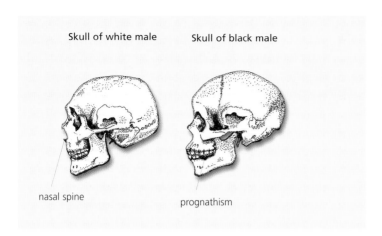

Skull of white male   Skull of black male

nasal spine

prognathism

opposite right A: Pubic symphysis of an 18-year-old. B: Pubic symphysis of a 60-year-old.

left Two skulls showing differences between biological groups.

human affinity. Also, the bone around the upper part of the mouth, called the maxilla, tends to project outwardly, a feature called prognathism.

Mongoloids exhibit far more prominent cheekbones, known as the cygomatics. It is this characteristic that gives the face a more flattened, rounded appearance. In some cases, ancestry can be suggested by the teeth, but here, too, human variability plays a great factor. The most notable dental characteristic exists among the

below Cultural and biological variations found among humans.

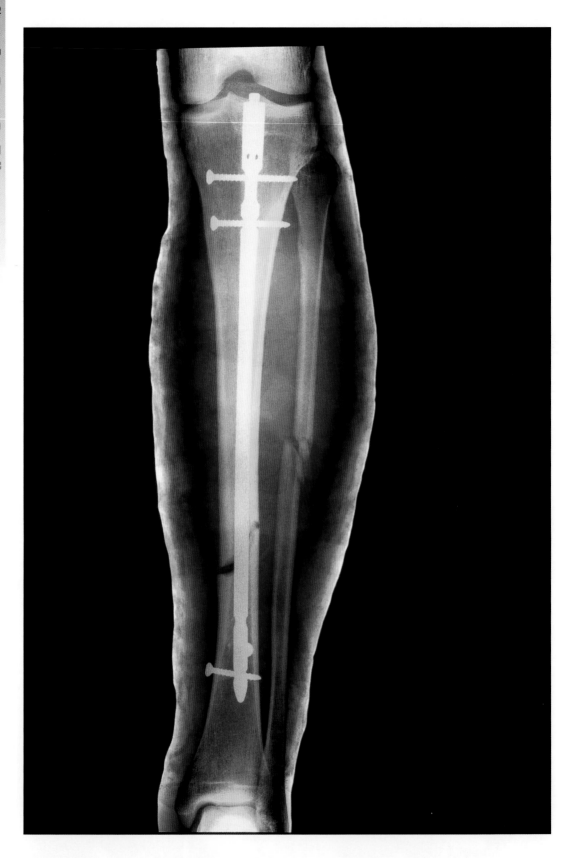

Mongoloid group, where a "shovel-shaped" indentation in the back of the upper front teeth may be viewed upon careful examination.

Due to the high level of influx of individuals within any given region, caused by global migration, this aspect is often the most difficult to assess; not all biological groups have been studied statistically to assess particular bone traits. Additionally, the admixture of characteristics due to intermarriage adds to the difficulty of arriving at a firm conclusion in this respect.

Stature

This aspect of the biological profile may be determined accurately by measuring the long bones, such as those of the legs and arms. An anthropologist can calculate the height of an individual by applying the total length of the bones to a mathematical equation developed from studies conducted upon skeletons of known stature. However, ancestry and sex should also be taken into account, because these factors influence the equation used, due to the variations in physical proportions of differing affinities. The result of the calculation will give an approximation of the height, allowing the investigator to compare the details with those of missing persons, or to verify the details of the possible victim. However, as people age, they shrink slightly, a factor that is taken into account when assessing the age of the individual at death.

When a body is found fragmented because of intentional mutilation or as a result of an explosion or a high-speed impact, such as occurs in an air disaster, anthropologists have developed mechanisms from which the stature can be assessed, by measuring only portions of arm and leg bones. In the case of an incomplete skeleton, if the vertebral spine is present, the height may be estimated. It can also be determined by measuring the bones that form the palm of the hand, called the metacarpals.

Individual characteristics

Once complete, the biological profile is compared with the characteristics of the alleged victim or those of known missing persons. Some police forces maintain a computer network with other jurisdictions, allowing access to a database of missing persons. By utilizing this information, anthropologists can trace and request antemortem radiographs (X-rays) and medical records from hospitals and medical offices that have treated the victim. In some instances a positive identification may then be achieved by matching characteristics observed in the remains with those noted in the records; in the event that the results are inconclusive, a DNA test can be used to gain a positive identification.

If radiographs are available, the remains are X-rayed and the results compared with the original material. The anthropologist will look for similarities in the internal structures of the bones, old fractures, and slight differences in the shapes of particular bones, the latter being an element of human variability. In this way, a positive match can often be achieved.

In conjunction with X-rays, medical records may also clarify whether the person suffered from a medical condition that had a direct effect on the bones. In the forensic field, bone pathologies may sometimes be

opposite X-ray showing fractures of a lower leg. A pin has been inserted and held into place with screws to help with the healing process.

encountered, although many of the afflictions that are evident on ancient remains taken from archeological sites are comparatively rare in modern populations. This is particularly true of tuberculosis and syphilis, in part due to advances that have been made in the medical treatment of these diseases. Conditions such as osteomyelitis, a bone infection caused by a pus-producing bacterium that enters the body through breaks in the skin caused by injuries, or by direct introduction into the bloodstream, may be readily detected in forensic cases. This particular condition is quite prevalent in intravenous drug users and causes bones to lose their normal shape by "swelling" and producing additional bony growths.

Orthopedic pins, which may have been used to correct prior traumas, are sometimes found among human remains. In such cases, medical data and X-rays may also assist in confirming the identification of the individual whose body once contained them.

Bone fractures heal over time, but usually scar tissue remains upon the affected bone. Damage caused by fractures may also be traced through medical records and X-rays, as was the case with a female skeleton found in Oklahoma. The examining anthropologist noted that the bones of the lower spine exhibited compression fractures typical of those caused by automobile accidents. The search of a database of missing persons established a positive match of the characteristics of the bones, and the woman's medical records indicated that she had indeed been involved in a car accident prior to her death.

X-rays continue to be used worldwide, aiding in the identification of human remains; however, the use of computer tomography scanning (CT scan) has become a modern tool within the forensic field. This technology utilizes a series of x-ray beams simultaneously, which are detected electronically, allowing the computer to produce a 2D cross-sectional image, with more specialized equipment being able to create 3D images. Although in the past this technology has been used solely for clinical purposes by medical doctors and dentists, its application within the forensic field has become popular for a variety of reasons

right A: Tibia without alteration. B: Tibia with squatting facets.

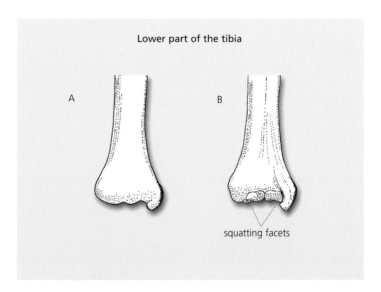

Lower part of the tibia

A

B

squatting facets

(see Chapters 5, 6, and 7); among these is the fact that the technology enables images to be compiled quickly and in excellent quality, allowing any observations to be made in more detail. With a multislice CT scan (MSCT), the number of images is increased with less time involved, but the quality of the images is maintained.

Additionally, this technology allows the remains to be examined by forensic pathologists and anthropologists without the need to open the body during the postmortem examination. Due to social and religious beliefs in some cultures, it is not possible to examine the remains within the framework of an autopsy; furthermore, bodies may also need to be buried within a short period of time, sometimes as little as 24 hours. A CT scan can help to meet these expectations; however, this technology is costly and not yet accessible globally by forensic specialists.

Another factor that can aid the identification of a person are particular alterations to certain bones, due to specific and habitual actions that put stress upon the body. One example is the use of squatting as a regular means of resting. Practiced for a protracted period of time in a habitual manner, squatting can cause the bones in the top of the foot to push up against the lower part of the tibia, commonly known as the shinbone. In the process, a mark may be created in the form of facets upon the shin bone.

Additionally, it may be possible to ascertain whether a person was right- or left-handed by examining the bones of the shoulder blades, since, in some cases, those from the side habitually used will exhibit arthritic changes over time.

When a person has suffered growth arrest because of an inadequate diet, or as the result of a prolonged disease, X-rays of the shinbones will show a series of transverse white lines. These are known as lines of arrested growth and, if measured, may provide information as to when the retardation of the growth process occurred. To illustrate this, a case was brought to the attention of an anthropologist in which the remains consisted of a skeletonized body, where some of the bones were fragmented. These were arranged in anatomical order, and it soon became apparent that they represented the incomplete skeleton of a child. When the bones were X-rayed, growth arrest lines were observed. This information and the characteristics of the child were forwarded to the investigator assigned to the case. The presence of growth arrest lines was a piece of information that helped to solve the case, since the child in question had suffered from neglect.

The same condition can apply to the teeth, which may suffer underdevelopment as a consequence of poor diet and disease. In cases of arrested development, teeth may exhibit a series of transverse lines, indicating a condition called hypoplasia. It is possible to estimate the time of developmental alteration by measuring these lines.

A further aid to positive identification occurs where the dentition of an individual has been altered by dental work, such as fillings, crowns, and bridges, or where dentures are worn. A forensic odontologist compares the teeth with antemortem dental records, which may result in a successful positive identification.

Close relatives of the deceased can also play an important role by allowing their DNA to be compared with the DNA of the individual in question—this can be extracted from the bones or teeth. Molecular biologists can test and compare the samples to determine a positive match.

DNA and forensic odontological analysis are the most common methods used worldwide in order to arrive at a positive identification.

Traumas and cause of death
The determination of the cause and manner of death rests upon the opinion of the forensic pathologist. However, where bones are involved, a forensic anthropologist may also assist, most frequently with reference to assessing sharp or blunt-force trauma, gunshot wounds, and, occasionally, strangulations. In situations where the bone has been fragmented, this professional can reconstruct the remains, and then proceed to make the required interpretations.

Sharp-force trauma

Sharp-force trauma can be defined as force applied to a narrow surface. In some crimes, sharp instruments such as knives, ice picks, scissors, and screwdrivers are used to damage the internal organs. These items are easily accessible within the household, and are frequently a weapon of choice; what is more, these tools do not raise suspicion when carried in a public area, as they can be easily concealed within clothing or a bag. When a person is killed by stab wounds to the chest area or to the back, bones are often damaged by the instrument as it enters the body. This damage can indicate the events that transpired during the murder. The bones most likely to present marks as the result of a stabbing are the ribs; here, the intervention of the forensic anthropologist is of utmost importance, as it is this professional who, with osteological knowledge, will place the ribs in anatomical order and assess when possible the number of stab wounds that affected the ribcage. The type of damage in each instance, such as hinge fractures, when part of the bone is lifted by the force of the blow but it is still attached to the body of the rib, or puncture wounds, when the tip of the weapon, as in the case of knife tips, strikes the bone and leaves a distinct puncture, may be assessed. Additionally, when the bones are placed in anatomical order, the cut marks may indicate the angle at which the wounds were delivered. Following these procedures, a careful examination can be completed by both the pathologist and the anthropologist, and may result in the determination of the type of instrument used. Here, the experience of both professionals can be key to a successful interpretation; in some cases, the cuts may be examined under a light or scanning electron

below CT scanning uses X-rays to produce cross-sectional images of the body; this allows the scientists to view internal body structures that can aid in the identification process.

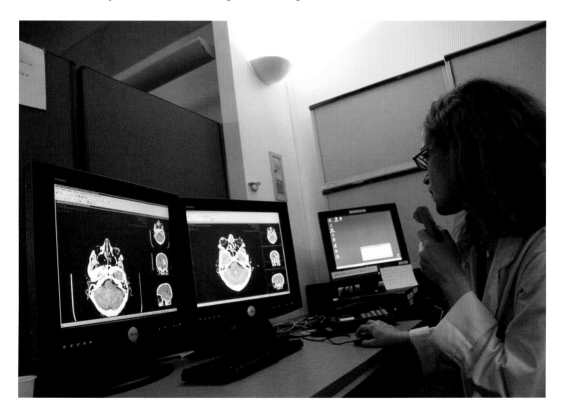

right A forensic scientist analyzes a garment with bloodstains. This type of investigation is caried out in cases of sharp-force trauma.

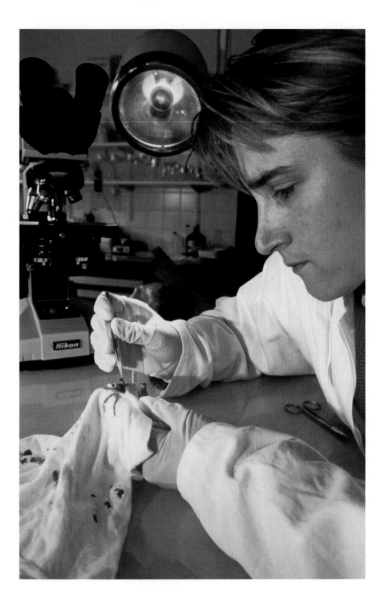

microscope (SEM) to gain further insight into the morphological characteristics of a particular wound.

Other sharp instruments used are meat cleavers, axes, and machetes. These are far bigger weapons and not easily concealed, yet are still used frequently in many homicide cases; machetes in particular are often a weapon of choice in rural areas of Latin America, simply because in many instances they are easily accessible due to being a common agricultural tool, or used in landscaping activities. The individual patterns and characteristics of the damage that these weapons cause are distinctive to the trained scientist, including, for example, cuts caused by a cleaver, which result in a narrow and sharp entrance wound, whereas machetes may create fracturing upon the bone. Moreover, the heaviness and sharpness of the blade of each particular instrument causes different effects. For instance, a dull machete will tend to splinter the bone instead

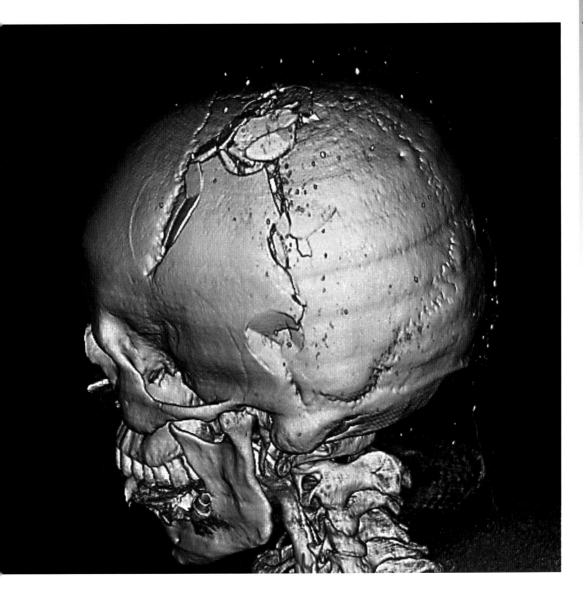

of slicing through it or cutting completely through a section of the victim's body.

In cases of dismemberment, many tools such as electric and hand saws may be used, depending upon what the perpetrator has nearby at the moment of the crime, and during its aftermath.

In murder cases, it is also important to determine whether cut marks were inflicted just before death. If they were, the cuts will have been made on "green" bone, meaning that the bone had not dried as a result of death. In this circumstance, the area of the bone that suffered the cut would have bent either outward or inward depending on where it was inflicted, a characteristic not seen in dried bone. The need to identify the nature of such cuts and how they were produced is of vital importance in a forensic investigation, because it serves to establish the sequence of events that occurred. In some instances, a killer may try to conceal the identity of the victim's body after it has been buried

above A colored 3D computed tomography (CT) scan of a fractured skull. The injury is due to an assault. There are multiple depressed fractures, part of the skull has been pushed inwards and fragmented into small pieces, and there are also radiating fractures.

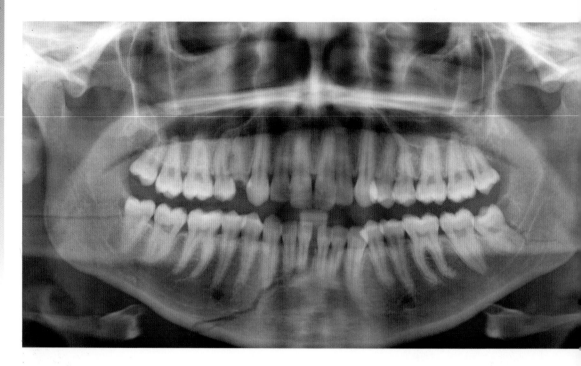

above X-ray of a mandible from a young female. Two radiating fractures can be seen in the bone, at right and bottom left. The injuries were a result of blunt-force trauma.

or hidden for some time. Having retrieved the body, the criminal may cause further damage by mutilating the remains during their dismemberment and disposal, leaving marks that are characteristic of those caused after the bones have dried.

Blunt-force trauma

Murder cases frequently involve the use of blunt instruments, characteristically low-velocity implements such as hammers, gun butts, or baseball bats, which create damage over a large surface area.

The amount of damage caused in such circumstances will depend on the force applied, the number of times the victim was struck, the angle from which the blow was delivered, and which kind of instrument was used. A blunt instrument is commonly used to produce damage to the head, whereupon fractures of the skull will radiate from the initial blow, with fragments possibly being driven in toward the brain; such radiating fractures are caused by the kinetic force of the blow, which dissipates as the radiating facture develops. By following the radiating fractures, the anthropologist can determine the sequence of events where multiple blows have been delivered.

However, blunt-instrument traumas can be misleading, since a blow to the body may cause enough damage to the organs to cause death, although the bones involved may receive very little damage in the process. This is particularly so in the chest area.

Gunshot wounds

Gunshot wounds damage internal organs, but in its trajectory through the body a bullet may cause deformation and shattering of the bones. Assembling the fragments of bone allows the trajectory of the bullet to be determined, as well as the locations of the entrance and the exit wounds.

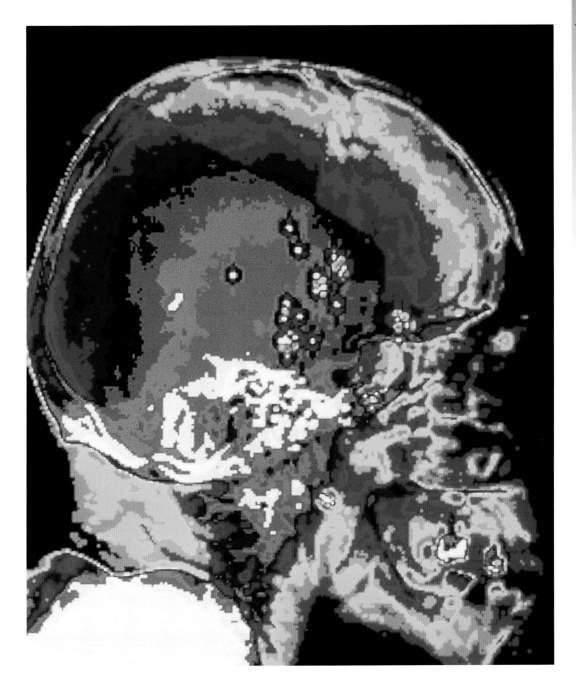

If the bullet is not present, either within the body or at the crime scene, its caliber may still be deduced by assessing the damage caused to the bones and the size of the wounds. This determination must be conducted by experts in ballistics, as many variables exist with respect to such wounds, including the manner of the elasticity of the tissues in question, the type of bones involved, and the angle of impact. The angle of the victim's body in relation to the gun may also be determined by the effect of the bullet, or bullets, upon the bones as it, or they, passed through the body.

above A computed tomography scan showing lead shots (blue spots) in the head as a result of a shooting accident.

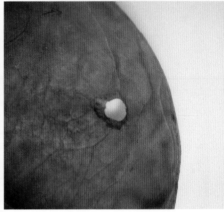

left A skull exhibiting blunt-trauma and radiating fractures.

top A skull shattered by a bullet wound.

above A bullet entry wound seen from the inside of the skull.

The entrance wound is generally smooth and small in comparison to the exit wound, because the forces created by the bullet as it passes through the body push bone fragments and soft tissue in front of it. A large, and usually bevelled, exit wound results, especially in the case of gunshot wounds to the head; such wounds will also cause radiating fractures as the force of impact dissipates through them. In some instances, the force is sufficient enough to separate large sections from the skull. Aside from the damage sustained by the bones, gunpowder may be discovered on the entrance wound, and lead particles may be observed inside the body when it is X-rayed.

Because gunshot wounds require assessment from a variety of professionals, such cases always involve the participation of the forensic pathologist, with the cooperation of forensic anthropologists and ballistics experts, in order to accurately assess the circumstances surrounding the death, and the type of gun used.

Strangulations

In many cases, manual strangulation produces damage to the hyoid bone, a small bone located in the upper part of the throat, just beneath the base of the tongue. In adults, this bone may fracture, but in children fractures of the hyoid are rarely observed, since the bones of young individuals tend to be quite flexible. Additionally, with respect to juveniles, the hyoid bone is composed of various sections that have not yet fused together; as such, when analyzing these bones, care must be taken to confirm that they are actually broken, and not simply a case of unfused sections.

above An assortment of bullets comprising different calibers.

left The delicate hyoid bone can easily fracture during strangulation.

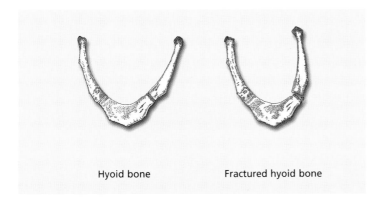

Hyoid bone   Fractured hyoid bone

John G. Haigh

By 1949, John G. Haigh had already been married, divorced, and convicted of theft, forgery, and swindling. His criminal tendencies had led him to serve a number of prison terms. However, these events were a far cry from the life that one would have expected him to lead as the product of a strictly religious and highly moral upbringing. Throughout his childhood and adolescent years, he attended church, rarely went to parties, and kept very much to himself.

During the mid-1930s, Haigh moved to London, where he committed himself to a life of crime. He was set on the idea of attaining wealth and the comfortable position in life that he felt he deserved. He dressed stylishly and was fastidious about personal hygiene.

Haigh's first murder victim was William McSwann, a business partner. After an evening of drinking, they made their way to 79 Gloucester Way, where Haigh bludgeoned McSwann to death. After the murder, Haigh placed the corpse in acid, and when the remains were dissolved fully, he disposed of the residue in a sewer. Meanwhile, Haigh informed McSwann's parents that their son had moved away temporarily, and for several months he supplied them with forged letters, supposedly from McSwann himself. Almost a year later, he murdered McSwann's parents in the same manner and subsequently took control of their assets while posing as their son. He continued committing murders using a similar modus operandi.

In early 1949, while staying at a hotel in South Kensington, London, Haigh met Olive Durand-Deacon, a 69-year-old widow. She mentioned to Haigh that she was developing a business idea and would appreciate his opinion. A few days later, she arranged to visit Haigh's workshop in Crawley, West Sussex. The workshop had been designed to facilitate conversion work, which entailed the breaking down of materials in strong acid, a business in which he insisted there was money to be made. Upon her arrival at the workshop, Haigh shot the woman in the back of the head, removed her jewelry and fur coat, and dumped her body into a drum full of acid.

Upon the disappearance of Mrs. Durand-Deacon, residents of the hotel raised the alarm. Haigh was questioned by the police, but denied knowing anything about it, saying that although they had arranged a meeting, she had not turned up. The police were

left John G. Haigh arrives at his trial handcuffed to a policeman.

below Police remove drums of acid for analysis from Haigh's workshop where Mrs. Durand-Deacon's remains were found.

right Mrs. Olive Durand-Deacon, whose body was disposed of in acid.

below right A wax figure of Haigh at Madame Tussaud's Chamber of Horrors in London.

suspicious of Haigh's statement and checked to see if he possessed a criminal record. When this proved to be the case, they paid a visit to his workshop. They discovered a variety of items, among which were documents relating to several different people, including the McSwanns, a recently fired .38 Enfield revolver and ammunition, and a receipt for the cleaning of a Persian lamb coat.

Haigh was certain that he was in the clear, because he believed that if there was no body to be recovered, the police would be unable to build a case against him. Then his plans fell into turmoil when, in a moment of over-confidence, he admitted to the police that he had indeed murdered the woman, but that only sludge remained.

The police, accompanied by a forensic pathologist, Dr. Simpson, returned to the workshop. There they discovered, aside from the sludge, 28 pounds (12.7 kilograms) of fat, eroded bone fragments, part of a left foot, several gallstones and a set of dentures. The body of Mrs. Durand-Deacon was positively identified by her former dentist upon examination of the dentures.

Haigh became popularly known as "The Acid-Bath Murderer." He was sentenced to death and subsequently executed in the summer of 1949. While he was in prison awaiting execution, a wax model was produced of him for display in the Chamber of Horrors exhibit at Madame Tussaud's Wax Museum in London.

Elmer McCurdy

Elmer McCurdy had tried a variety of trades, including mining and plumbing, and he had seen service in the army. But he finally opted for a career outside the law, his specialty being armed robbery.

During the fall of 1911, McCurdy, in the company of fellow robbers, decided to steal a safe from a train that regularly followed a route down through Missouri and Kansas to Texas, known as the Katy Train. The safe was supposed to contain thousands of dollars in payments intended for Native Americans. They forced the train to stop at Okesa, Oklahoma, but made a crucial error and stopped the wrong train; all they recovered from the safe was $46 and some bottles of whiskey.

The robbers split up and, two days later, McCurdy happened upon a ranch in the Osage Hills, where he got drunk and retired eventually to a hayloft. The following morning, a posse caught up with him and a shootout ensued that lasted for about an hour. When no further sign of life came from McCurdy, the hayloft was checked and McCurdy was indeed found dead, killed by a .32-caliber gunshot wound.

McCurdy's body was taken to a funeral parlor in Pawhuska, Oklahoma, but when no relatives

opposite Elmer McCurdy in his casket.

opposite below The Katy train in the early 1900s.

right Actor Lee Majors who played Steve Austin in the TV series *The Six Million Dollar Man*.

or friends came forward to claim it, the undertaker embalmed the corpse with great quantities of arsenic, a practice that became illegal throughout most of the United States after the 1920s. Then he charged people five cents each to view the body of "The Bandit Who Wouldn't Give Up." Some five years later, two conmen turned up at the funeral parlor. One of them claimed to be McCurdy's brother and indicated that he wanted to give the body a proper burial in California.

Back in California, the two men coated McCurdy's body in wax. It then embarked on a long and interesting career in show business, passed from owner to owner, and used in various circuses and amusement parks.

The true nature of the wax-covered corpse was discovered when a crew filming an episode of the television series "The Six Million Dollar Man" was working at the Nu-Pike Amusement Park. While setting up a scene at The Funhouse, the crew removed a

dummy that was hanging from the ceiling and that had been painted with red phosphorescent paint so that it glowed in the dark. When one of the crew attempted to move the dummy, part of an arm fell away, exposing a bone.

The "dummy" proved to be a real mummy, and it was taken to the Los Angeles Medical Examiner's Office, where it was autopsied. Marks discovered on the groin indicated that the body had been embalmed, and many of the organs were in an excellent state of preservation, some retaining good pigmentation.

With the help of historians and information offered by people who had heard about the find, the puzzle soon began to come together. Although no medical or dental records were discovered, mugshots of McCurdy still existed from when he had been in jail many years before.

Forensic anthropologists Drs. Judy Suchey and Clyde Snow based their analysis on the prison records, and set about identifying

the body. Taking into consideration the shrinkage suffered by the body throughout the years, the facial features still closely matched the prison pictures. The height, taken by measuring the femur (the thighbone) was determined to be 5 ft and 8 in (1.7 m). The age was estimated by examining the characteristics of the pubic bone and the maturation of other bones, which indicated an individual older than 20, but younger than 35 at the time of death. McCurdy was 31 years old when he died. Additionally, a scar he was known to have had on the right wrist could still be detected. A positive match for identification was made.

In the spring of 1977, McCurdy was buried at Summit View Cemetery in Guthrie, Oklahoma, with hundreds of people in attendance. After the service, concrete was poured over the coffin to ensure that Elmer McCurdy had found his final resting place.

Dr. Carl Weiss

US Senator Huey Pierce Long dedicated his life to politics. He was Governor of Louisiana before being elected senator, a position he held at the time of his death.

Various US senators have died violent deaths while in office, including Senator David C. Broderick in 1859, Senator Robert Kennedy in 1968, and Senator Huey Pierce Long in 1935. The circumstances surrounding the latter's death remain a mystery. Dr. Carl Weiss, a respected physician, was widely considered to be the assassin but many speculate that Senator Long was accidentally killed by his own bodyguards.

What is known, however, is that on September 8, 1935, Weiss confronted Long at the State Capitol Building in Baton Rouge, Louisiana, whereupon gunfire ensued. Long was seriously wounded during the exchange, and Weiss died at the scene. Long was taken to Our Lady of the Lake Sanitarium. He had suffered a perforating wound of the abdomen but doctors at the hospital failed to notice the damage to Long's kidney. He died some 30 hours later from internal hemorrhaging.

No autopsy was performed on Long's body, and the proper authorities were not permitted to examine his corpse. The inquest into his death was ended abruptly by the Louisiana State Legislature and the inquest into Weiss's death was postponed as some of Long's bodyguards refused to testify. Additionally, no significant evidence went through a proper chain of custody at the time of the offence and therefore many of the artifacts that have emerged over the years are no longer admissible as evidence as their provenance cannot be accurately determined.

A number of different scenarios have been offered and widely debated. One version is that Weiss approached Long and shot him at close range with a .32-caliber pistol. Long's bodyguards responded immediately by firing upon Weiss, killing him almost instantly. Another version suggests that Weiss hit Long in the face, whereupon Long's bodyguards shot at Weiss, killing him. During the exchange of gunfire, however, Long was accidentally wounded by his own bodyguards. To cover up the incident and to protect Long's bodyguards from prosecution, Weiss' gun—the only incriminating evidence in the case—was removed from his car in order to frame him.

The Weiss family remained convinced that Dr. Weiss was not guilty of Long's murder. In 1991, 56 years after the event, and in an effort to resolve the case, Weiss' family requested that his body be exhumed, hoping for some clarity and understanding to be brought to light, and that his name might be cleared as a result. A team of forensic scientists led by Professor James E. Starrs of George Washington University exhumed Weiss' remains from Roselawn Cemetery in Baton Rouge. However, attempts to exhume Long's remains were blocked by his descendents.

To avoid disturbing the remains, the opening of the vault and the removal of the deteriorated casket that contained Weiss' remains were carried out meticulously. A portable X-ray unit was used on site to document the condition of the remains. The body was then transported to the Lafayette Parish Forensic Laboratory, where the forensic pathology work took place, and further X-rays were taken to locate any metal objects. Weiss' body was skeletonized and almost complete, with the exception of some bones that had become very brittle. Only a small amount of soft tissue and clothing remained. For the anthropological examination, the bones were transported to the Smithsonian Institution in Washington, D.C.

Forensic analysis revealed that the damage inflicted to the bones was consistent with the bullets found with the remains. The examination of Weiss' remains indicated that a minimum of 20 bullet wounds had affected his skeletal remains. It is also quite probable, however, that several other wounds were inflicted which had penetrated the soft tissues alone, leaving the bones unaffected.

The bullets' trajectories indicated that most of the shots were fired into Weiss from behind, although some of the bullets had struck him from the front in the chest area. Bullet wounds were also present to the head, and trauma evident upon Weiss' arms and hands were seen as consistent with defensive gestures that individuals make when under attack, such as shielding the face. Forensic analysis confirmed that Weiss had died as a result of receiving multiple gunshot wounds from a variety of different angles and weapons.

Despite the new forensic information in 1991 and the discovery of some missing police reports—including the pistol that had been owned by Weiss and a spent bullet—there is still no evidence that can accurately

determine whether Senator Long was killed accidentally by his own bodyguards or by Weiss. However, ballistic analysis of the firearm indicated that the bullet did not originate from Weiss' gun.

The intervention of forensic anthropology in this case shed new light into the death of Dr. Weiss, and leaves the door open for further investigations into the events in Baton Rouge over 65 years ago.

opposite Dr. Carl Weiss.

below Senator Huey Long who was shot dead at the State Capitol Building, Baton Rouge, Louisiana (**bottom**).

The Pig Farmer

Robert Pickton, a pig farmer based at Port Coquitlam, British Columbia, Canada, is considered to have been Canada's most prolific known serial killer. When the case against him came to trial, the authorities presented nearly 40,000 photographs and over 200,000 items as evidence. The court proceedings, which lasted several months, cost over $10 million dollars, making this case the longest and most expensive ever tried in Canada.

Vancouver's Downtown Eastside is known as a deprived sector. It is rife with drug and gang activity. Prostitution is a problem too, with many underage females addicted to drugs.

Over the years, females within the sex trade had disappeared; these events were sporadic, and seemingly without a discernible pattern which would connect them to a specific perpetrator and modus operandi. This problem was compounded by the fact that prostitutes do not always maintain contact with friends and relatives, making the exact places and times of disappearances difficult to ascertain. Although the list of missing women was growing, it was unknown if they were actually dead, and as such the investigation was slow in

above Accused serial killer Robert Pickton (R) is seen in an artist's illustration at BC Supreme Court in New Westminster, British Columbia.

right An out building at the Port Coquitlam pig farm belonging to Robert William Pickton.

below Workers searched through buildings and mountains of dirt and debris in search of human remains.

developing. Furthermore, the perpetrator did not strike on a constant basis, but instead sporadically, often with gaps of years.

The police did not take an active interest, as cases pertaining to prostitutes are often of little concern to the public, and as such are a low priority. Ultimately, the authorities began to investigate these cases, the corollary of which was rising media interest. The list of potential suspects included Gary Ridgway, the Green River Killer, who was later eliminated from the investigation. However, during 1998, an employee of Pickton's, Bill Hiscox, came forth, believing that his boss was responsible for the disappearances. His opinion

right A police investigator analyzes what may be human remains on the site of the Coquitlam pig farm.

was based on comments made by Pickton himself, and also on items belonging to females, including personal items and documents, which he had seen. But the investigation stagnated, and no arrest was made.

Subsequently, it was confirmed that in 1997 Pickton was charged with attempted murder against a prostitute; his farm was searched, yet no progress resulted. Meanwhile, the number of missing women continued to grow.

In 2002, Vancouver police announced that the Pickton pig farm was to be searched; murder charges were subsequently made against him on several counts. Contained within buckets, pigpens, a freezer, and also spread upon the surface of the ground were the remains of body parts. The condition of these remains was both skeletonized, and in varying stages of decomposition. Several thousand bone fragments, teeth, blood stains and hair traces were recovered and documented. Some of these finds were eventually used successfully within DNA analysis to produce positive identifications.

Forensic analysis determined that bones from cranial and post cranial regions displayed cut marks caused by a hand held reciprocal saw, as used to butcher pigs. Gunshot wounds were also noted on some of the remains. The recovered bone fragments were mixed within large quantities of animal bone, yet human remains were recognized and separated for analysis.

In 2007, the trial concluded with six convictions of second degree murder, as evidence was not sufficient to support first degree murder charges. A sentence of 25 years was given, with ineligibility for parole. The six victims connected to the trial were murdered subsequent to his 1997 attempted murder charge and the prior Hiscox testimony.

Although not all of the disappearances were resolved, it is believed that the killings spanned from 1983 to 2001, with the number of victims exceeding the 54 accounted for as missing from the area.

right Royal Canadian Mounted Police investigators move debris on the pig farm in 2002.

below Royal Canadian Mounted Police investigators officers and animal control officers prepare to check the farm.

3 Exhumations and Other Stories

above Destroyed buildings in Haiti following the earthquake in January 2010. Cadaver dogs may be used when searching human remains trapped within structures.

When it comes to forensic investigations, no two crime scenes are identical, and each case presents its own challenges and hurdles. Investigating a crime requires much organization, effort, and patience by the police, forensic team, and all those involved behind the scenes.

« Bodies have been discovered in the homes of individuals who killed to satisfy necrophilic urges, or who liked the taste of human flesh. Various parts of the deceased may be used to construct shrines, or kept as trophies. **»**

Depending on the country in which the investigation is being conducted, the organizational scheme and the titles of the people working on a case may vary. However, as a general rule, a person is assigned as the crime-scene coordinator and takes charge of the operation, overseeing the procedures at the scene, and ensuring that they are carried out correctly and meticulously. If they are not, the entire investigation may be botched and the case thrown out of court.

A criminal case involving a search for a buried body will often be prompted by information obtained from a previous investigation, or from a tip-off given to the police by an individual. Such a burial is known as a clandestine grave, because the body will have been concealed with the aim of keeping the murder secret.

When the site of the exhumation has been confirmed, the coordinator has to decide on the equipment and personnel required, taking into account the type of terrain in which the search is to be carried out. A team will be assembled from police officers and forensic experts. For an exhumation, the police will seek the help of forensic personnel trained in archeology, because the procedures they utilize during the recovery of the remains will be meticulous. Any evidence that may be present at the scene will be found and cataloged. The actual removal of the remains, especially when skeletonized, is facilitated by the forensic anthropologist. The loose bones will be lifted carefully from the burial site and subsequently packaged, a process that requires special techniques.

However, not all corpses are buried outdoors in clandestine graves; some may be concealed within man-made structures. Such cases pose challenges in recovering bodies, and the procedures used may differ, depending on individual circumstances. Additionally, in cases where buildings collapse, as during severe earthquakes, the recovery of human remains is normally conducted by emergency personnel but can also include forensic staff who can aid in the process, specially where the integrity of the bodies has been compromised.

Types of interment

Over time, humans have developed a variety of funeral and burial practices, depending on their individual cultures. Each social group, as archeology has shown, has its own way of disposing of its dead, with some rites being more elaborate than others. In some circumstances, geographical conditions have dictated these customs.

A good example of sumptuous burial practice is that employed by the pharaohs of Egypt. The custom of mummification began in Egypt over 5,000 years ago and was intended to preserve the rulers for the afterlife. Each body had its internal organs removed, the brain being extracted through the nose, and the remaining organs through a small incision in the stomach

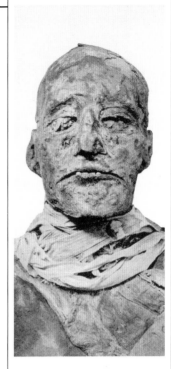

above The preserved body of the Egyptian pharaoh Rameses III.

below The mummified body from ancient Egypt.

above Depiction of the ceremonial embalming of Tutankhamen, Egypt.

region. Both body and internal organs were treated with natron (sodium carbonate), resins, oils, and spices to preserve them. Finally, the body was wrapped in over 1,000 yards (910 meters) of linen and placed in a sarcophagus; the organs were put into special containers known as canopic jars. Burial followed in a chamber within a pyramid, the construction of which had been started many years prior to the occasion. There, the pharaoh was left with jewelry and other items deemed necessary for the afterlife.

By contrast, some cultures in North America, such as the Inuit over 2,000 years ago, employed simple burial practices. In the northern latitudes occupied by these people, the permafrost prevented the digging of graves, so a body would be wrapped in animal skins and deposited on top of the ground. A few personal items of the deceased would be left alongside, covered with rocks. Some American Indian tribes placed the body on a scaffold, where it was left until it became skeletonized through the natural process of decomposition and the intervention of carrion birds and other creatures, which would consume the flesh. In some instances, removal of the flesh was accomplished with the aid of a sharp instrument. Once the body was free of flesh, the disarticulated bones were placed in a secondary burial site, a communal grave, called an ossuary.

Just as cultures around the world have developed different burial practices, within the forensic field, investigators are confronted not only with clandestine graves, but also, from time to time, with bizarre and unusual circumstances that require the removal of bodies from the most unimaginable places.

Unusual disposals

There are many instances in which the disposal and concealment of a body are unusual. Potential hiding places include septic tanks, crawl spaces, closets, refrigerators, interiors of walls, spaces beneath floorboards, abandoned buildings, and drums filled with concrete. In such cases, discovering the body may not be difficult because the remains are confined within a structure, but actual retrieval may pose problems.

Some murderers choose to leave the body, or bodies, in the house where they reside. Such was the case of John Wayne Gacey, from Illinois, who killed over 30 young people and disposed of some of the bodies in the crawl spaces of his house. Because the bodies were skeletonized when discovered and the bones were mixed together, a forensic anthropologist was called in to sort them out in order to determine the number of individuals present.

below Policemen recovering bodies from the crawl space beneath the home of John Wayne Gacy.

Additionally, bodies have been discovered in the homes of individuals who killed to satisfy necrophilic urges, or who liked the taste of human flesh. In such cases, the body of the victim is kept for a period of time and, eventually, is concealed in a variety of ways within the home. Various parts of the deceased may be used to construct shrines, or kept as trophies (see case study No. 9).

Some murderers go a step further when concealing bodies—for instance, by obtaining a drum, placing the body in it, and covering the remains with concrete. The removal of a body in such a situation may be very difficult, requiring the use of power tools, which may cause damage to the remains and obliterate marks that could be of great value in the forensic analysis. In such cases, specialized tools—including air chisels, which provide control of the depth of blast—are used to gingerly remove the remains. A body concealed under a concrete slab or asphalt poses a challenge as well, and heavy construction equipment, such as a backhoe, may be called in. This must be used with great care to retrieve the victim.

In the case of a septic tank, removal may require specialized equipment or ingenuity on the part of the search team. In one case of this type, the body of a man was dumped into a tank, where it remained for a few weeks. Upon discovery, the body was retrieved in an advanced state of decomposition, as were the remains of a woman's nightdress. The investigation revealed that a crime of passion had taken place. In another case, the body of a man was hidden in the septic tank of a house. Many years later, when tenants complained about the toilet backing up, a search was made of the pipes and the tank itself. In the process, bones were discovered, along with remnants of clothing. The body had remained there for nearly 15 years.

Searching for a clandestine grave

The search for a clandestine grave may be difficult if the area to be surveyed is large. Factors that may hamper the search are vast wooded areas with thick trees, rugged terrain, and the effects of the weather. Stormy conditions or frozen or flooded ground may delay the operation. The most efficient way to conduct a search is with a multidisciplinary team, comprising experts from a variety of fields, including police officers and independent professionals, such as dog handlers, forensic anthropologists, geophysicists, and aerial photographers.

Where and how to carry out the search are critical decisions, and modern forensic science has developed several instruments and techniques that aid the task. Consequently, investigators are able to find clandestine graves at a much faster and more reliable rate. Experiments conducted in Colorado by a group of professionals from different fields have proved the effectiveness of the multidisciplinary approach in searching for a clandestine grave. In part, their research was based on the recovery of buried pig carcasses. Pigs were chosen because the animal is by far the best substitute for the human body in terms of weight, amount of corporal hair to surface ratio, and the quantities of fat and muscle in the body. The graves were located by a variety of methods, and the reliability of the recoveries assessed. The multidisciplinary approach was found to be the best technique, since it takes into account that the circumstances surrounding burials may vary depending on the location. This group of professionals created a voluntary organization called NecroSearch International, which assists in the search for, and retrieval of, missing persons, and also gathering evidence from within the grave and the surrounding area. This organization has enjoyed an excellent success rate (see case study No. 10).

Locating the bodies

Among the new techniques employed in the search for clandestine graves is the use of geophysical techniques as ground-penetrating radar (GPR). This handy portable instrument gives a reading within a few minutes, saving time and money. It uses the electric properties of the soil to identify disturbances in the ground, but will also penetrate snow and water. Ground-penetrating radar was of great help to a group of scientists wanting to recover tissue from those who died from the

below Ground-penetrating radar in use.

Spanish Flu in the early 1900s. The aim was to analyze the tissue in the hope of identifying the organism responsible for the deaths of over 40 million people worldwide. The graves chosen for this study were in Norway, near the North Pole. Radar allowed the precise location of the graves to be plotted and, as a result, they suffered minimal disturbance. This was important, since the tissue recovered could still have been contaminated with the virus.

GPR is most effective on level terrain, so alternative methods must be considered when searching hilly or mountainous areas; one option is to employ trained dogs, often called "cadaver dogs", which are normally handled by the police force involved with the case. As a body decomposes through the effects of cellular breakdown, many different odors emanate from it, depending upon the stage of decomposition. Even if only the bones remain, the scent will be perceived by a well-trained dog. Indeed, a cadaver dog may be able to locate a body that has been dead for hundreds of years.

Different types of dog are used for this particular task, such as German shepherd dogs and bloodhounds. The latter are particularly good at searching for bodies submerged in water. However, they are not the best of swimmers, so the dog carries out the search from a boat and, for added safety, wears a life preserver. As the boat moves through the water, the dog sniffs at the surface. Once it has sensed where the body may be, it will jump into the water, to be followed by scuba divers.

below German shepherd dogs and bloodhounds are trained to aid in the search for human bodies.

left Police searching the grounds
with the aid of a metal detector.

Another way to locate a burial site is to take soil gas readings. This form
of detection can be undertaken when close to a potential burial site, since
a decomposing body will produce methane and other gases.

When a large area is being covered, aerial photography may also be
utilized. This is most effective when the area under investigation has been
photographed before, allowing the topography to be compared. Other
alterations due to the burial, such as the movement of vegetation or
structural alteration to the landscape, may also come to light.

Geological observations made through archeological techniques at
a site will seek to discover soil alterations. These alterations come about
because soil comprises different layers, each with specific
characteristics. When a grave is dug, the different layers of soil are

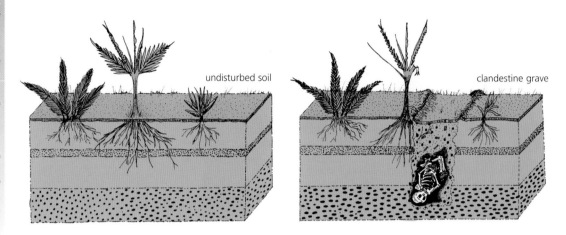

undisturbed soil

clandestine grave

mixed, causing changes in color and texture compared with undisturbed areas nearby. Soil texture may be judged with a metal probe. As the soil is removed and subsequently returned to the grave, the degree of compaction changes. It becomes "looser" after it has been disturbed, and this is detectable with the probe. However, such a tool must be used by an expert, because if it is inserted too deeply in the ground and with haste, it may touch the body below and cause damage. If soft tissue is present upon the remains, the damage produced by a probe can resemble the entrance wound caused by a firearm.

below The skeletonized body of a person who was flung into a pit.

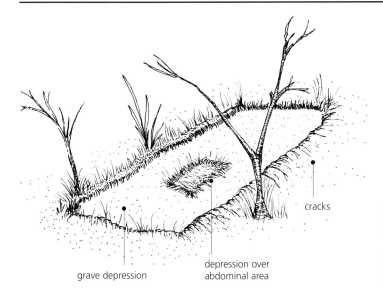

cracks

grave depression

depression over abdominal area

opposite A comparison of undisturbed and disturbed ground strata and roots.

left Features visible upon the ground, characteristic of a clandestine grave.

Tell-tale signs

Since a body will take up a significant amount of space within a pit, there will be surplus soil displaced around it. There may also be footprints at the grave site, left by the individual who dug it, providing further evidence for the investigators to use.

Decomposition of the body plays another important role in the appearance of the grave. As the organs start to decompose in the abdominal cavity, the soil that lies over it will begin to sink. This creates a depression that is often readily observed. Additionally, the entire area that was excavated will sink as the soil settles back into place, and signs of cracking will appear around the edges of the grave. However, in sandy areas, because of the characteristics of the material, the visual search for clues is virtually impossible.

In addition to changes in the soil, the surrounding vegetation may have been altered, its pattern differing from the vegetation nearby. If much time has elapsed since the burial took place, the regeneration of the vegetation may not be apparent. The speed of this regeneration varies depending on local climatic conditions. For example, in tropical zones, plants grow far more rapidly than in temperate areas, to the extent that within a few weeks, a great deal of new growth may be evident. Quite the opposite may be the case in colder regions, where plants grow at a slower rate. The relative rate of regeneration of the vegetation surrounding the grave may assist in determining the time of burial.

Obtaining the time of burial is crucial to the resolution of any murder investigation. It will indicate whether the burial was initiated soon after the murder, or some time afterward. The roots of plants that happen to be regenerating, or newly established plants with shallow roots on top of the grave, will indicate to a botanist the amount of time that has passed since the soil was disturbed. If a body is buried close to a tree, eventually its roots may reach the spot where the body is located. By examining the growth rings within the roots, the botanist can determine how long they would have taken to reach the body.

All of these methods and indicators are available to forensic scientists when seeking clandestine graves. In any given case, those chosen will depend upon individual circumstances.

Exhumations

Persons directly involved in an exhumation must wear protective clothing. This ensures that the area under investigation is not contaminated inadvertently, and protects the health of the investigators. As a general rule, investigators don hair caps, and men with beards or mustaches wear facial protection. Disposable coveralls are worn, as are gloves and shoe protectors.

At every crime scene, minute items of trace evidence are found and subsequently cataloged. Such evidence includes strands of human hair, animal hair, blood spots, dirt, vegetation, fingerprints, sawdust, and a variety of fibers. Such elements are usually transferable, meaning that they may be borne away from the crime scene just as easily as similar items may be carried there by anyone involved in the crime.

For example, a criminal may take his time in hiding a body by burying it in a remote wooded area. However, when the clothing of the perpetrator is examined at a later date, minute traces of dirt and vegetation may be found to link him with the scene of the burial, since certain types of vegetation and dirt are specific to microenvironments.

Hair strands are easily shed and transfer readily to other elements, including human bodies. The same is true of many fibers. During the early 1980s, several young boys were murdered in the city of Atlanta, Georgia. After a long investigation, carpet fibers found on a victim's clothing were matched with those from the apartment of the chief suspect, as well as from his car. These discoveries, together with other evidence collected, led to the suspect's conviction.

Although various types of evidence may suffer from the passing of time, as well as other factors, such as the weather, when carefully sought and properly retrieved, they may tell of events that have transpired and help to identify criminals. Depending on the type of evidence discovered, each item will be sent to an appropriate laboratory for analysis. Before this happens, however, the evidence is properly bagged, sealed, and labeled. Every time it changes hands, it must be signed for, thereby ensuring continuity in the chain of custody of each item, so that its whereabouts are known at all times. This ensures that the evidence cannot be altered or tampered with following recovery, an issue often suggested by defense attorneys.

Carrying out exhumations

At every exhumation, a space will be designated next to the grave where the scientists will work, preventing any disturbance of the grave site itself as work progresses.

A datum point should be selected prior to starting the exhumation, as it is from this reference point that all archeological measurements are taken. This point should always be a permanent fixture, such as a tree or structure of permanence, or created manually by using a metal pipe.

The removal of the soil is accomplished by lifting layers of 10 in (25 cm) at a time. Soil from each layer is passed through sieves with different sizes of mesh to extract any evidence that may have been left behind. For example, an item such as a cigarette butt, which may seem insignificant, must be collected and cataloged, since traces of saliva may be present upon it, aiding the identification of the culprit. The number of soil layers

opposite Human hair strands as seen through an electron microscope.

Colored Scanning Electron Micrograph (SEM) of **opposite**, nylon stocking fibers; **above**, linen; and **left**, cotton fabric.

right Police unload sieves and shovels to search for the mutilated remains of Denis Nilsen's victims.

removed will depend upon how deeply the body has been buried. In some cases, the depth can be considerable—often 3 ft (1 m) or more. The quantity of soil that must be removed will also have a bearing on the amount of time that will be needed to complete the exhumation.

The time needed to work a grave site properly will vary with the condition of the remains. Several factors play a role in the decomposition or preservation of human remains. Buried bodies can be said to be protected from the elements, and therefore the remains will be largely unaltered. This is true to a point, but if the soil happens to be acidic in nature, the corpse will tend to decompose more rapidly. Such is the case in tropical regions, where acidic soils and high temperatures, combined with high humidity, may cause a body to decompose very quickly. Such conditions can be so extreme that at archeological burial sites, graves sometimes do not contain any human remains at all due to their total disintegration. Under these circumstances, in more recent burials, the remains may be partially disintegrated and skeletonized within five years. On the other hand, in temperate zones, especially in areas where there are severe winters with long periods of ground freezing, the processes of decomposition will be slowed to a minimum.

Another factor that can affect a body after burial is saponification. This can occur if the remains are buried in an area that is moist, or are directly exposed to water and kept free of air for a period of time. During saponification, the fatty tissues of the body are turned into a grayish waxlike substance called adipocere. In the case of a fetus, the quantity of fatty tissue may not be sufficient for the remains to become saponified.

When a body has been left for a period of time under water, and provided the flesh is not consumed by animal action, it will eventually saponify.

An example that illustrates saponification well is the case of the Belgian cargo ship, Mineral Dampier, which sank in the China Sea during the mid-1990s, after colliding with a Korean ship. It took divers over a year to recover the bodies, because of the freezing waters and the depth of the wreckage. Those recovered exhibited different degrees of adipocere formation, the last bodies to be retrieved possessing the highest quantities. If the adipocere is in contact with the bones, when the remains are brought to the surface and exposed to the air, it will dry and adhere to them. Apidocere is very difficult to remove from bones without damaging them in the process.

Whether the body has saponified or not, the natural process of decomposition will always take place. The human body decomposes at various rates, causing the gradual loss of all its soft tissues, including the connective tissues such as tendons and ligaments. Eventually, the body will become skeletonized, leaving only the bones with no connections between them.

A condition contrary to saponification is mummification. When a body is buried in an arid environment, and better yet, in a hot sandy area, eventually it will become mummified. This is because the soft tissues will dehydrate rapidly, inhibiting the bacterial growth associated with the decomposition process. When this occurs, the internal organs are well preserved, and diseases from which the deceased may have suffered can often be assessed. Additionally, scars, tattoos, and other identifying characteristics are well preserved on the dry skin, which eventually adheres to the bones. This may be seen in the naturally mummified bodies that are buried in areas of South America, such as northern Chile, where conditions are ideal for the process to occur.

left A clandestine grave in process of excavation with remains and clothing visible. A scale is set next to the excavation for photographic purposes.

Removal of the body

When the remains within a grave are skeletonized, they may be fragile and fragmented, and it is the responsibility of the forensic anthropologists to collect the bones in a proper manner. The body must be exposed completely before it can be lifted from the grave. This is accomplished by the use of such small tools as dental picks, bamboo sticks, paintbrushes, and hand trowels, all of which provide a controlled means of exhumation.

Paintbrushes are handy for removing soil from bones, but their use is avoided when clothing is present, since any loose bristles may contaminate the environment of the scene. As the body is gradually exposed and prepared for removal, its various parts are bagged, labeled, and sealed according to each body section in the same manner as items of evidence. The bones are then placed in boxes to protect them while they are transported to the laboratory for analysis.

However, after the remains have been removed, the excavation continues. A further 10 inches (25 centimeters) of soil is removed in case small bones or any other evidence may have been left behind. Also, by looking at the stratigraphy (layering) of the soil, it may be possible to determine if another grave lays beneath the first one.

As with any crime scene, the procedures carried out and the items found must be recorded by means of photography and video, and a written account is also maintained. Careful adherence to these procedures ensures that the investigation can be reviewed with accuracy at a later date, and also used as evidence in court.

below An almost skeletonized body is visible through clothing.

It is essential to record the condition and position in which a body was found, and also any items that were discovered with it, such as a wallet, personal identification card, or clothing. When personal documents are found with a body, it must not be assumed that they belong to the deceased. Various possibilities exist, such as the intentional placing of false documents to confuse investigators.

The position of the body is of great importance, because this information can provide a basis for the reconstruction of events leading up to its burial. Since, initially, the means of murder or concealment will be unknown to those investigating the case, the perpetrator will often give a distorted account of what transpired when questioned by the authorities. Some individuals will try to frame others for a murder and give contradictory testimony when questioned. However, accurate information obtained from the grave itself may shed light on the real circumstances of the case.

All of the processes conducted during the search and retrieval of the victim's body are appropriately recorded through police photographs and sketches; the latter are produced based upon measurements taken during the exhumation.

Cemetery graves

In some instances, it may be necessary to exhume a body from an established grave within a cemetery, usually due to doubts about the cause of death. A forensic anthropologist may be called upon at the time of the exhumation, in case the body is skeletonized and handling of the bones is necessary during removal of the remains. However, the exhumation will not require the same level of preparation and types of procedure employed in the case of a clandestine grave.

There are various other reasons why the exhumation of remains from existing graves may be requested—for example, to solve a mysterious death, or for repatriation, or because there is a need for reburial. Such was the case with the Ox Hill Battle Field soldiers, whose remains were discovered when the Centerville fortification in Virginia was bulldozed; anthropologist Dr. D. Owsley from the Smithsonian Institution was called in to handle the skeletal remains.

In such cases, a body may be either totally skeletonized or well preserved. This will depend upon the type of coffin used, the environment in which the individual was buried, whether the remains were buried in the ground or sealed in a vault, and also whether the body was embalmed. Embalming is a means of preserving a body and may be achieved by a variety of methods. Today, it is often employed to allow time for making funeral arrangements, and also to give the deceased a composed and restful pose for viewing.

In the past, embalming was accomplished by using arsenic, as was the case in the United States until the practice was outlawed in the early 20th century (see case study No. 5). Now, embalming is achieved by injecting the body with formaldehyde, through incisions made to reach the carotid artery. As several gallons of formaldehyde are injected into the circulatory system, the blood is pumped out through the jugular vein until the fixing liquid has replaced the blood completely. This halts the process of decomposition by destroying the bacteria responsible for tissue decay.

An embalmed body may remain without visible decay for many decades. However, if moisture enters the coffin, mold and bacteria growth will induce the decomposition process.

Ernesto "Che" Guevara

Ernesto "Che" Guevara de la Serna was born on June 14, 1928, in Rosario, Argentina. His family enjoyed a comfortable lifestyle, and the young Ernesto graduated with a doctorate in medicine from the University of Buenos Aires.

Guevara's political ideals were Marxist in nature and eventually were channeled toward taking direct political action against dictatorships and capitalist imperialism. His ideology took him to many countries, including Cuba, where he fought alongside Fidel Castro to overthrow the Batista regime during the late 1950s.

In late 1966, his attention was focused on Bolivia, where he was fighting to undermine its government. He had organized a communist guerrilla movement, aided by other South American nationals and Cubans. Nearly a year later, approximately a third of Guevara's force had been killed. The Bolivian government offered a $4,200 reward for his capture, and moved to arrest any individuals who aided the guerrilla movement.

The guerrillas suffered from many illnesses and eventually retreated toward a village called La Higuera. There they were attacked by the Bolivian Army, and during the battle Guevara lost many more of his men. Eventually, he and the

remainder of his force succeeded in withdrawing from the area. On October 8, at Valle Serrano, they were cornered and subjected to a heavy attack, causing further losses, and many soldiers were wounded. The casualties included Guevara, who sustained wounds to his right arm and leg. Late in the afternoon, his force was overpowered, arrested and returned to La Higuera.

The next day, Guevara was executed by Bolivian soldiers at the schoolhouse where he was being detained. He was shot in the legs, arms, and thorax. Then his corpse was flown by helicopter to Vallegrande, where he was fingerprinted and embalmed. His hands were cut off as proof of his identity. The death certificate indicated that the cause of death was severe hemorrhage as a consequence of the wounds inflicted upon his thorax.

On October 12, Guevara's brother, Roberto, arrived in Bolivia to collect the body, but he was told that it had been cremated and the ashes taken to Vallegrande.

The whereabouts of Guevara's body remained a mystery until July 1995, when Bolivian General Mario Vargas Salinas indicated that he had participated in a mass burial near Vallegrande in Central Bolivia, close to a dirt airstrip, and that a grave there actually contained Guevara's body.

An extensive search for the site ensued, carried out by Cuban forensic personnel and the Argentine Anthropological Forensic Team. They relied upon ground-penetrating radar, digital imaging, indications of soil alterations, and historical and antemortem accounts of the events to locate the grave. The search took over two years to complete.

Finally, in 1997, the mass grave was located and forensic archeological techniques were applied. For security reasons, the scientists slept inside the grave

top Ernesto "Che" Guevara.

left Cuban leader Fidel Castro giving a speech before the National Assembly.

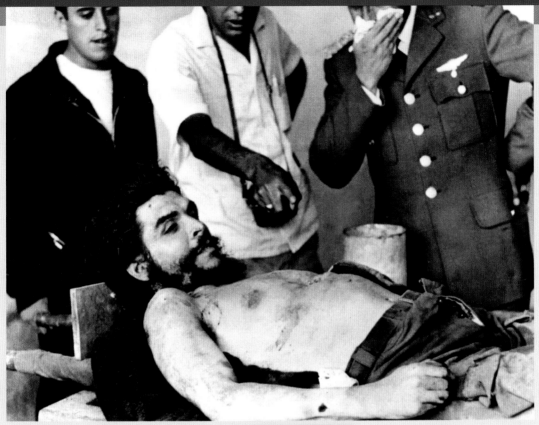

above The body of guerrilla leader Ernesto "Che" Guevara shortly after his execution.

left Skeletal remains of "Che" Guevara laid out for the identification process.

alongside the bones, which were found with such personal effects as clothes, shoes, and belts, and in the case of Guevara, his jacket, which contained some tobacco. Although the personal effects helped in identifying the occupants of the grave, the antemortem information available to the investigators confirmed their analysis. The bone characteristics of each skeleton, including old lesions, together with the cranial superimposition and dental records confirmed identification. The fact that Guevara's body lacked both hands and exhibited traumas to the chest and legs made his remains particularly noticeable. Apparently his comrades had all been killed by gunshot wounds to the head, as evidenced by their shattered craniums. No genetic work was necessary, as there was sufficient evidence to confirm their identities.

More than 30 years after his execution, Guevara received a hero's welcome in Cuba. His remains were put on display, then buried in July 1997 in a mausoleum at Plaza Ernesto Che Guevara in Santa Clara, Cuba.

Jeffrey Dahmer

During the summer of 1991, 39-year-old Jeffrey Dahmer was arrested at his home in Milwaukee, Wisconsin. His one-bedroom apartment was then searched for human remains.

N o one would have suspected anything, had it not been for a handcuffed man found running from Dahmer's apartment building. He informed police officers that he had barely escaped death at the hands of a man who was living at the Oxford Apartment Complex. As a result, the police officers agreed to investigate the apartment.

Over the previous 13 years, Dahmer had carried out a series of murders upon men whom he had picked up, and in some cases offered money in return for photography sessions. Once in his apartment, he would drug and strangle them. Then he performed sexual acts upon the corpses, after which they were mutilated.

During some of the killings, Dahmer had carried out a form of lobotomy on the victim, by drilling a hole in the head and injecting muriatic acid into the brain, causing almost

above Jeffrey Dahmer before Milwaukee County Circuit Court, 1991.

below left View of Oxford Apartments where Dahmer lived.

below Inside Dahmer's apartment.

opposite Forensic personnel removing evidence from Dahmer's apartment.

instantaneous death. He would photograph the process of killing, to view later for his own pleasure.

Although upon initial inspection Dahmer's apartment looked clean and tidy, an overpowering smell filled the air. What was discovered inside the apartment was truly shocking. He possessed pictures of the victims, some in erotic poses, which continued through the killing process and culminated in their eventual dismemberment. One complete skeleton was discovered in his bedroom, and concealed in his closet were soft human body parts in a state of decomposition.

A decomposing head and other body parts were discovered in his refrigerator. Contained in the freezer were additional heads and body parts, and other body parts were discovered in a barrel. In his statements, Dahmer claimed that he engaged in cannibalism.

Dr. Bennett, from the University of Wisconsin, was asked by the Milwaukee County Medical Examiner's Office to carry out a forensic analysis of the seven skulls found, including that of the complete skeleton. Some were decomposing with flesh still adhering to them, whereas others had been cleaned completely, having been boiled to remove the flesh, then prepared afterward. Dahmer's eventual objective had been to create a shrine incorporating the skulls of his victims.

The anthropological analysis indicated that some of the skulls exhibited a small hole in the upper forehead region, where muriatic acid had been introduced. Additionally, the investigation confirmed that all the skulls were male, and of white, Asian, and black affinities. Information gathered by the police during their investigation was matched with the anthropological analysis in an attempt to identify the victims.

Each skull was also analyzed by a forensic odontologist, Dr. Johnson, who recorded the dental work that each individual had received. With an indication of the possible identities of the individuals, he proceeded to compare his analysis with their dental records and, as a result, he was able to make positive identifications.

Dahmer was convicted and sent to Columbia Correctional Institute in Portage, Wisconsin, to serve a combined prison sentence of 957 years. During the fall of 1994, three years after beginning his jail term, he was attacked by a fellow inmate while carrying out janitorial work. Dahmer's head was crushed during the assault, and he died as a result of the injuries he sustained.

Thomas Luther

The search for a clandestine grave may provide a considerable challenge for forensic investigators, especially if the murderer has taken great pains to conceal the remains of the victim. In this respect, Thomas Luther was no exception.

Elder   **Luther**

L uther had recently been released from prison, after serving a 10-year sentence for sexual assault. Some of his fellow inmates said that he bragged about murdering someone, and that the corpse would never be found.

One day in the spring of 1993, 20-year-old Cher Elder from Denver had argued with her boyfriend, Byron Powers. After leaving him, she decided to head for Central City, Colorado, where she spent part of that evening at a casino. A surveillance camera in the casino captured images of Cher in the company of Thomas Luther, who happened to be an acquaintance of Powers. They left the casino together some time after one in the morning, and this was the last time Cher was seen alive.

Upon her disappearance, her father contacted the Lakewood Police Department in Denver. Investigations were initiated, but Cher was not found; meanwhile, time was ticking away.

Subsequently, a team of forensic scientists, called NecroSearch, was

Woman missing since gambling trip

Suspect implicated 2nd time

Luther's three victims resembled his mother

opposite top left and right
Photographs of Cher Elder and her convicted assailant Thomas Luther.

opposite below Elder was last seen alive at a casino in Central City, Colorado, accompanied by Thomas Luther.

asked by the police to assist in the search for Cher's body. Following a tip-off, the authorities suspected that the body was most likely to be concealed in the Empire Valley region, west of Denver. This made the search somewhat difficult, since the Empire Valley embraces an extensive wooded area of hills and rocky terrain.

The forensic team brought a multidisciplinary approach to the search, and was assisted by trained dogs, in addition to aerial surveys of the area. In 1995, as a result of further information received by the police, the investigators concentrated their efforts upon a steep hill and initiated a ground search. They began looking for geological clues, such as soil alteration, but the ground was frozen and they had to halt the search temporarily.

Meanwhile, Powers had been convicted on a separate charge and, as a result, he began bargaining with the police in the hope of being given a lighter sentence. He told them he knew exactly where Elder's body was hidden. When the investigators returned to the same hilly area they had visited previously, they discovered that the body was just a stone's throw from where they had stopped searching.

Once the clandestine grave had been located, the team began to excavate the area utilizing archeological techniques, employing small hand tools initially and carefully sifting the soil. Full recovery of the body was achieved, the remains being identified as those of Cher Elder following comparison

with her dental records. Her remains showed that she had been shot in the head at close range. The excavation was undertaken with such care that plant roots, which had grown into the body while it lay under the ground, were also recovered.

Subsequently, a botanist performed a microscopic analysis on the roots. Their characteristics suggested that they were nearly two years old, which assisted in establishing the time of burial. This information helped to secure the conviction of Thomas Luther, who was given a 48-year prison sentence.

Luther spared death sentence

Zachary Taylor

President Zachary Taylor, a native of Kentucky, was the 12th president of the United States. He was best known for his time in the United States Army, during which he was involved in several military campaigns. He was hailed as a hero of the Mexican War of 1846, and was considered as being "regular army," earning the affectionate nickname of "Old Rough and Ready."

No one suspected that President Taylor's term of office would end in an abrupt manner. However, on July 4, 1850, after laying the foundation stone for what was to be the Washington Monument, he dined on some raw vegetables, fresh fruit, and buttermilk, then became gravely ill. He had developed the symptoms of gastritis and severe diarrhea.

Five days later, Taylor died, aged 66. His sudden death has been the subject of considerable conjecture—as to what really occurred, and the most probable cause of his death.

Because Taylor's symptoms were consistent with those associated with arsenic poisoning, there was a strong possibility that he had been murdered. Arsenic occurs naturally in minute quantities in the sea, soil, and the human body itself, but when present in large quantities, it becomes poisonous. If Taylor had died of arsenic poisoning, traces would be found in his fingernails, hair, and bones. With the permission of his family, the body of President Taylor was exhumed in June 1991 at the Zachary Taylor National Cemetery in Louisville, Kentucky. However, due to the small size of the mausoleum, the

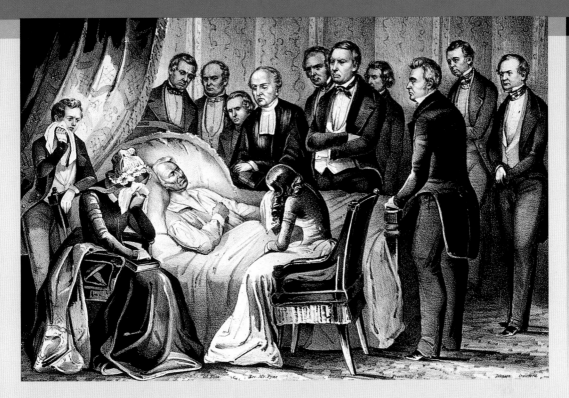

coffin containing his remains was transported to the office of the county medical examiner. The body was skeletonized, but with hair, and the finger and toenails present.

It was the task of the late Dr. William Maples, a forensic anthropologist, to remove bone, hair, and nail samples, which were to be analyzed to assess the levels of arsenic present. Samples were sent to the Oak Ridge National Laboratory and the Kentucky State Laboratory, and both produced identical toxicological results. The traces of arsenic found in President Zachary Taylor were minute, ruling out arsenic poisoning as a possible cause of death. To this day, the real cause remains a mystery.

opposite above Zachary Taylor.

opposite below General Zachary Taylor leading American troops into battle at Palo Alto during the Mexican-American war.

above Zachary Taylor on his death bed at home, surrounded by friends and family.

below Arsenic, which in large, or small repeated doses, can prove fatal.

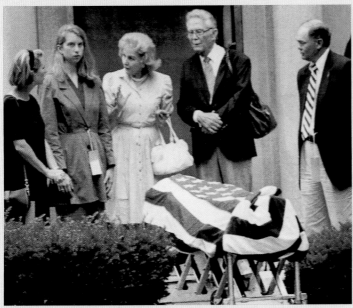

left Relatives of U.S. President General Zachary Taylor at his exhumation in Kentucky in 1991.

4 Surface Bodies: The Outdoor Setting

Not all murder victims are buried in clandestine graves or concealed by other means. Some are disposed of in the open, usually in rural or semirural areas, far from where they are likely to be discovered, but seldom within city limits or even small communities. There they can lie for long periods of time, their whereabouts unknown until their remains may be chanced upon many years later.

In many cases, murder victims whose remains have been deposited in quiet country areas, even if close to a major highway or a site that is visited regularly by people, are not discovered until many years later. However, it must be kept in mind that not all bodies discovered in such circumstances are victims of foul play. Some individuals may have died of natural causes or as a result of an accident. Bodies discovered in such situations are often encountered by someone hiking, hunting, or simply walking a dog.

Regardless of the apparent cause of death, the site must be investigated fully, and any items found near the remains must be analyzed thoroughly. In cases concerning seemingly natural causes of death, where the body has been reduced to bones, it may not be possible to determine any other factors that could have led to death.

Cases of this kind generally require the participation of forensic anthropologists with archeological training, since often the remains will be partly or completely skeletonized. Additionally, this type of situation is affected by a variety of factors that will alter the condition of the remains and any evidence present, which may cause problems during the investigation. A forensic anthropologist may assist in locating and delineating the area to be searched, then aid the recovery of the human remains, as well as reconstructing the events that transpired before and after death.

Taphonomy is taken into account when analyzing the changes that may have occurred at a crime scene, caused by such factors as climate and geography. These include amounts of local rainfall, temperature, types of local scavenger and carrion bird, the local terrain, and soil type. When preparing a search, several considerations must be taken into account before the investigation is initiated. How large is the area? What is the best way to reach the site? Is it rough terrain? What type of equipment may be required? Is it snowing? Such considerations influence the degree that taphonomic factors may have played in altering the scene.

« The maggots develop by consuming the soft tissue, their numbers often reaching such a high level that the term 'maggot mass' is used. Such a mass may cover an entire adult body and consume it at an incredible rate. »

Climatic factors

When a corpse and associated evidence have remained exposed to the elements for some time, it is likely that the body and related artifacts will have been altered and displaced, causing the true context of the scene to become confusing to the investigator. In such circumstances, a multidisciplinary approach will be of benefit during the investigation, resulting in a more accurate reconstruction of the events that have transpired since the individual died, or was left at the scene.

Human remains that are left upon the ground without any protection will tend to decompose more rapidly than if they were buried. This is due to

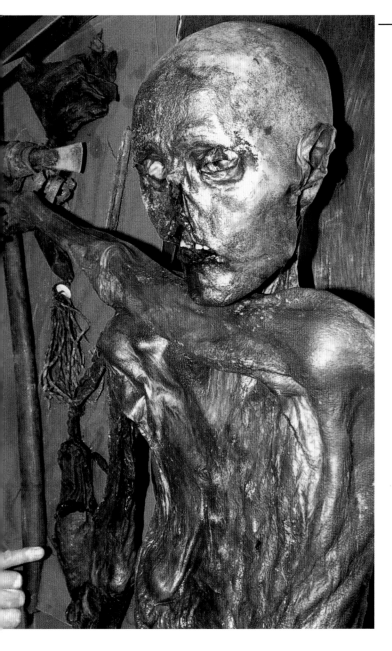

left The well preserved body of Ötzi the 5,300 year old iceman, probably one of the oldest mummies in the world.

the effects of temperature variation, humidity, scavenging by animals, insect activity, and soil type at the scene. These factors vary depending on the geographical location of the search. For example, tropical regions produce elements that lead to extreme decomposition, whereas the opposite is the case in cold zones.

In areas where extremely cold temperatures exist for most, or all, of the year, with constant winds and dry conditions, as found in polar regions and high mountain ranges, a body could undergo a process of natural mummification, commonly referred to as "freeze drying." In this situation, as in the case of the artificial mummification method practiced by the ancient Egyptians, a body will retain well-preserved soft tissues, which aid assessment and analysis when attempting to identify the remains. An excellent example of freeze drying would be the well-preserved body of a man who became known as "Ötzi." It had lain

left George Mallory, who died on his expedition to Mount Everest. His body (below) was found 75 years after his death.

undiscovered for over 5,000 years in the mountains on the border between Italy and Austria. The body had been preserved so well by the wind and the cold that tattoos were still visible upon his skin. Scientists who examined his remains were able to determine the presence of intestinal parasites, and could distinguish certain items of clothing. Another example is the British mountaineer George Mallory. In 1924, while leading an expedition to Mount Everest, Mallory went missing. After 75 years, however, his body was discovered in an excellent state of preservation, with the skin still present, and the clothing surviving so well that the makers' tags were still visible and legible on some garments.

Desiccation of the body tissues may also occur in windy, arid areas, even if the region is not a cold one. If animal activity is relatively low, as might be the case in such deserts as the Sahara and the Atacama area of northern Chile, human remains may be well preserved with very little or no dispersal at all.

below Thick vegetation
in a rainforest, which can
impair a forensic search.

However, excellent preservation of the body and accompanying artifacts is not usual. In most cases, the local climate will play an important role in the decomposition process. As an extreme contrast to cold areas, tropical regions experience relatively high temperatures and humidity; factors that, when combined, will greatly accelerate the decomposition process. Nonetheless, even in tropical regions, a body that has been left in the shade will decompose more slowly than remains exposed to full sun.

Decomposition of bodies

In addition to changes brought about by climatic factors, many crime victims may be dismembered and the remains spread over a wide area by the culprit. These may decompose at a faster rate because large areas of soft tissue are exposed to bacterial invasion.

Regardless of how quickly or slowly a body decomposes, once a person dies, flies will be attracted to the body in a matter of minutes under most climatic conditions—other than extreme cold. The types of fly vary from region to region. As a general rule, the metallic blue and green "bottle" flies commonly seen where garbage has accumulated, are among the first insects present. As soon as the flies arrive, they deposit their eggs in natural openings in the body where it is moist, such as around the eyes, nostrils, and mouth—the last two being the most attractive areas because odors emanate from them. If the body happens to be naked, eggs will also be deposited at the genitals and anus.

Where open wounds have been inflicted on a body by some form of weapon, areas of soft tissue will be exposed, and in many cases additional eggs will be deposited in these areas, too. As the maggots hatch, they cluster and feed first in such regions. If a body is discovered at this stage, maggots found covering an area that is not a natural opening indicates that trauma has been inflicted on that part of the body.

The maggots develop by consuming the soft tissue, their numbers often reaching such a high level that the term "maggot mass" is used. They may cover an entire adult body and consume it at an incredible rate. As they feed on the body, the maggots progress through a series of stages, called instars, during which they shed their skins as they grow. In the final stage, they become a hard-cased pupa that is dark in color. When ready to pupate, the maggots leave the body and burrow into the earth, from which, eventually, new flies emerge.

opposite A female bluebottle fly laying eggs on raw beefsteak.

center Maggot mass capable of consuming soft tissue at a very fast rate.

below A blowfly pupa case, from which a fly will emerge within 3 to 5 days.

right The presence of drugs, such as cocaine, may be detectable in body tissue long after death.

If there are a large number of maggots present in a body, these may leave track marks on the ground when they leave it to pupate, they can leave track marks on the ground. A trained entomologist or anthropologist can identify such tracks, preventing them from being mistaken for marks caused by the body being dragged to the area. Investigating scientists appreciate the need to collect entomological evidence found in relation to a body. When analyzed in the laboratory, such evidence may indicate the possible use of drugs and may aid in determining the time of death. Maggots will absorb any drug that may be present in the remains by consuming the soft tissues. Even pupal casings, left after the flies have hatched, will contain traces of the drug. A good example of this is a body that was discovered on the east coast of the United States. It was partially skeletonized with desiccated tissue harboring maggots. The body and clothing showed no indication of foul play. A toxicological examination was carried out on the maggots, and it was found that the individual had consumed a large amount of cocaine. As a result of the entomological evidence, the cause of death was determined.

Assessing the time and place of death

The actual time of death may be difficult to assess from entomological evidence, because of the many variables involved in each particular case, and because the exact time when the flies laid the eggs will not be known. That is why it is referred to as the minimum time of death. However, the information that may be gained from an entomological analysis can be of significance to the investigation. An entomologist, knowing the species of fly, the stage of maggot development, and the nature of the prevailing weather conditions, can estimate the length of time that the maggots have been present upon the remains. As a result, it may be possible to indicate the time of death with a reasonable degree of accuracy.

The presence of flies can also indicate whether a body has been buried and subsequently exhumed. Not all flies can enter the ground and survive, but some, such as the coffin fly, can do just that. Being subterranean insects, coffin flies most typically affect remains that are buried. When they are present upon human remains discovered above ground, this usually indicates that the body has been exhumed from its original burial place. An experienced forensic entomologist would be able to interpret this evidence and uncover the story behind it.

Scavengers and other animals

Other insects will also feed upon decaying human remains. Some, such as ants, cockroaches, and lice, prefer flesh. Certain beetles, such as dermestids, consume the dried tissue, in effect "cleaning" the bones of flesh. Even butterflies have been known to feed upon the decomposing fluids of corpses. However, insects are not the only creatures that take an active role in the disintegration of the body; scavengers also play a part and, in the process, may disturb evidence at the scene.

If a body has been covered at the time of concealment, or even if it is in a shallow grave, this may not provide enough protection when scavengers are present. A body in the process of decomposition will emit odors that attract animals, and they will quickly locate and gain access to the body.

These animals may cause severe damage to the scene by destroying the indicators that would help in the interpretation of the events associated with the death of the individual, not to mention causing alterations to the remains. The distribution of scavengers depends upon geographical, climatic, and ecological factors. In North America, such scavengers include alligators, coyotes, rodents, bears, wolverines, wolves, vultures, and crows. By contrast, in an area such as the United Kingdom, the effects of scavenging can be comparatively minimal, since there are relatively few scavengers to be found in rural and semirural areas. Such animals, if present at all, would usually be rats, mice, foxes, and carrion birds, such as crows.

below The bone of a forearm splintered by animal gnawing.

bottom Lower torso and legs discovered under vegetation.

left Carrion birds, such as crows, can have an impact on the skeletonization process of a corpse.

The activities of rodents are known to cause damage within the area of the death site. They will consume facial tissue, regardless of whether it is fresh or has dried out, and will also gnaw at bones, leaving clear tooth marks. Rodents may also nest in the chest area of a victim, constructing the nest from pieces of clothing, paper, hair, and vegetation.

Larger mammals tend to attack the facial region, the stomach area, and the buttocks. These sections of the body are easily accessible, and the last two contain large volumes of flesh. Bones may also be consumed, but some will only be accessible after the body has been dismembered. In the case of long bones, the ends are preferred because the spongy bone structure is easier to chew. Such activities will leave tooth marks on the bones, indicating the type of animal that was present and allowing it to be tracked. Tracking the animal may help to find further remains along its trail, or within its droppings.

Clothing may hamper the action of animals, but this will depend upon the type of clothing worn by the deceased, and in some regions the time of year will be a factor in this. It is not unusual for anthropologists to work with remains that are nearly skeletonized in both hands and facial area, but with the remaining tissues still decomposing under clothing.

Carrion birds aid the skeletonization process by consuming exposed soft tissue. In the same manner as maggots, they tend to attack the natural openings in the body, as well as any wounds.

When climatic factors are combined with the effects of insects and scavengers in a tropical region, a body may be nearly or completely skeletonized within two weeks, if all of these factors are present at the highest possible levels.

It is also possible to find that a body has been altered by scavenging even when it is inside a structure, such as a house. A scenario frequently encountered by investigators is the discovery of the remains of an individual who lived alone and has since passed away. In such cases, the body may have been decomposing for a considerable period of time and may exhibit the marks of scavenging rodents or a domestic dog that was once a pet.

The search for clues

When conducting a search, a forensic investigative team will assess the type of topography, amounts of local rainfall, and also the varieties of animals common to the area. With this information, the search can be oriented to take into account the factors that are most likely to have altered the scene since death.

When the body has been modified and displaced, the remains are usually discovered in a very fragmented state, being spread over a wide area. The task of the anthropologist is to determine the original location of the remains, because this is where the majority of the evidence may be discovered. Because of animal activities, the original site may not be easy to locate. Among the clues that the anthropologist looks for are strong odors associated with stains on the ground. Such stains are caused by corporal fluids, which are released as the body decomposes.

In conjunction with other investigators, the anthropologist will assess the types of animal present and the feeding patterns indicated by the scavenged remains. The numbers of scavengers present in the area may be possible to ascertain since, for example, certain animals, such as coyotes, travel in packs of as many as 20.

As the animals take turns at feeding on the remains, the corpse may be moved a great distance. Such was the case with a man who had been decapitated. When the authorities arrived at the crime scene, the head was missing, and a wide search ensued to locate it. Eventually, it was discovered that the missing head had been removed by coyotes and taken several miles from the original site. It is because of such situations that knowledge of the scavengers in the region, the numbers that move together, and their eating patterns is of great value. The longer a body has been exposed, the more scattering by dismemberment will occur, and the longer it will take to search for the remains. As a result, a search can cover an extensive area and involve great amounts of time and manpower.

Knowledge of the trails that animals use and the ability to follow their tracks, or at least identify them, are important for several reasons. When a body begins to decompose, the gums start to disappear and, as a result, the teeth become loose. As they loosen, they tend to fall off, and when animals scavenge the body, some teeth may be consumed, which in turn are passed with the animals' droppings. The identification of the animals involved is important, since by recovering the appropriate droppings, or "scats," they may be examined to recover the missing teeth, which are then compared to dental records. This search may not always be successful, but it has proved positive on several occasions.

If rodents are known to be in the area, the anthropologist will seek out their burrows, or structures where they may nest. Rodents tend to take small bones, such as those of the hands and feet, in addition to small personal items, such as rings.

Birds are also known to play a part in displacement of human remains. They may remove fibers from clothing, or even hair from the body, using these materials for building their nests. This has been observed in Britain, where rook nests have been found to contain human hair.

Being unaware of the behavior of the animals present at the crime site means that considerable amounts of remains and evidence will be lost, and the scene itself may be misinterpreted. A good example is that of mountain lions in the United States who have been known to kill humans. After dispatching its victim, the cat may cover the remains with vegetation and return later to retrieve them. In the meantime, if the body happens to be discovered, the death may be misinterpreted as the action of a person rather than an animal.

The effect of topography

As a search party moves through an area, the topography is another vital factor to consider. The techniques required to search for a body in an area that is relatively open and flat, with little greenery, are different to those needed to survey an area that is heavily wooded with rugged terrain.

below The mountain lion, a native of the Americas, conceals his kill with branches to return at a later date.

In addition to considering the topography, the team will also have to take into account the amount of precipitation. Rainfall tends to splatter dirt upon skeletal remains, and small bones, such as those of the hands and feet, are likely to be buried as the soil is splattered on them. An experienced anthropologist will recognize this possibility and bear it in mind during the search. Additionally, hilly areas should receive consideration, because bones will tend to roll down them, and if heavy rainfall is a factor, the remains are likely to be washed down steep slopes, along with associated items from the scene.

Locating and identifying the body

When dealing with concealed human remains, investigators may employ cadaver dogs to locate bodies that are well hidden or well dispersed. The forensic team may also perceive odors themselves if their search takes them close enough to the body. Additionally, since flies are attracted to odors, a swarm hovering over a specific area could well lead to the discovery of human remains. Other techniques that may be applied include the use of metal detectors, which can assist greatly in the location of personal effects and other evidence that may remain at the scene and in the immediate area.

A search may be facilitated or hampered, depending on the topography and vegetation of the area in question. An example of extreme adverse conditions would be those that exist in the world's tropical regions. Such zones tend to be endowed with thick vegetation and extremely rugged topography. Machetes may be needed to clear the growth as a search progresses. Because the vegetation and undergrowth can be so thick, the recovery of small bones may be very difficult to accomplish.

As the team works through an area, when remains are spotted they will be marked with flags. The idea is to map the findings, allowing the subsequent reconstruction of events, as well as assisting the anthropological analysis by recording the location of each body section. At any scene, it may not be known initially how many bodies are present.

The actions of a killer may play an indirect role in dispersing the bones, which may be shattered by a heavy blow from a blunt instrument, or by the effects of a large-caliber firearm. As the tissues decompose, such bone fragments will be "freed" and will fall from their anatomical positions. This, combined with scavenging, will produce many small pieces of bone for the anthropologist to work with. Although most of the remains at a scene may be recovered eventually, it is rarely possible to reassemble a complete skeleton.

The recovery operation

The anthropologist may take several days to reassemble the remains once they have been found. Much attention will be given to confirming whether any bones have been duplicated, since this would indicate the number of individuals involved.

Many people go missing every year, but not all of them are reported. A large number of recovered bodies are assessed to determine their physical profiles, but positive identification may never result because no one comes forward to inquire about them. In such instances, the remains must be kept in storage in case more information is gathered or, if the remains are incomplete, in the hope that they may be matched with future recoveries.

Sometimes, a murderer may decide to leave the body for a considerable period of time in a particular spot. Subsequently, some of the remains, having become skeletonized or been dismembered, may be transported by the killer to an entirely different location. It is important for police forces from different jurisdictions to retain and make available any data that enables the effective cross-referencing of information relating to the missing persons in their areas, in addition to any cases involving unidentified human remains. In this way, connections may be made, and may lead to the realization that two separate cases from different jurisdictions involve the remains of only one individual and the actions of one criminal (see case study No. 13).

As with buried remains (Chapter 3), the processes conducted at the scene are comprehensively recorded through photographs and archeological sketches.

below Rescue personnel working at the scene of an earthquake disaster.

Jeffrey Dahmer

Jeffrey Dahmer led an introverted, but tense, teenage life, which was tinged with alcohol abuse. Eventually, he became a serial killer and cannibal, embarking upon a rampage of death and brutality that lasted for 13 years.

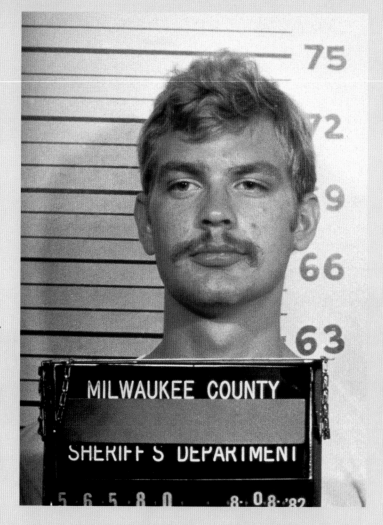

His first crime was committed in 1978 at his parents' home, in the semirural area of Bath, Ohio. The victim was Steven Hicks, an 18-year-old male hitchhiker whom Dahmer had picked up. Dahmer had invited Hicks to his parents' house, since both were away at the time.

After he had had sex with Hicks, Dahmer did not want him to leave so he decided to kill Hicks by striking him on the head with a barbell, after which he strangled him to death. Then Dahmer proceeded to dismember the corpse with a bowie knife. He then placed the body parts in plastic bags and buried them in a wooded area behind his parents' house.

Some time later, Dahmer decided to dig up the plastic bags. He crushed the remains with a sledgehammer and scattered them in the same wooded area. This crime was not discovered until his final arrest in 1991 (see case study No. 9), by which time he had murdered a total of 17 men.

Following the discovery of Dahmer's activities and his subsequent arrest, the police obtained a statement from him. Dahmer told them about his crimes, including his first murder in 1978. Prompted by the information provided, the area in Bath was carefully searched, and a variety of artifacts, as well as

animal bones and fragmented human bones, were discovered. The authorities decided to call in physical anthropologists from the Smithsonian Institution in Washington, D.C., to assist in their investigation.

The material was transported to Washington, where scientists proceeded to analyze it. One of the first steps was to separate the human bones from the nonhuman remains discovered in the same area. The latter were of domestic animals, such as chickens and cows, and wild fauna native to the region.

Eventually, it became possible to analyze the pieces of human bone, which numbered over 250 and which were, in many cases, in an extremely fragmented condition. The first step was to determine whether they had originated from more than one body. The investigators found that no body part was duplicated, indicating that they came from one individual only.

The human bone fragments exhibited cut marks and severe fragmentation, in addition to damage that had been caused by exposure to the elements over

many years. The conclusions reached by the scientists closely matched Dahmer's recollections.

Individual characteristics of the recovered victim matched those of Hicks in age, sex, and height. Additionally, radiographs taken of the victim at some time prior to his death proved of great assistance, enabling a comparison to be made with those taken after his death. Even though the remains that were analyzed were in an extremely fragmented condition, a positive identification of the victim was possible.

opposite Jeffrey Dahmer after his arrest in 1982.

above Policemen searching for clues at Dahmer's boyhood home in Bath, Ohio, where bloodstained clothing belonging to Steven Hicks was discovered.

below left An official uses a metal detector to search for remains. An assortment of both human and animal bones were recovered.

Green River Killer

From 1982 to 1998, dozens of young women were murdered in the Seattle/Tacoma area of Washington in the United States. All of the victims were involved in prostitution, who worked along the "Strip," a red-light district near the Sea-Tac-Airport.

The investigation into these serial killings began near Kent, Washington, after two boys, making their way over the Peck Bridge spanning the Green River, spotted the body of a naked woman with a pair of jeans wrapped around her neck. The subsequent forensic examination indicated that she had been strangled. Soon after, another naked female body was found on a sandbar, and eventually many other victims were discovered in a variety of locations nearby.

As the number of cases grew, the Green River Task Force was formed. This organization encompassed several police jurisdictions, not only because bodies were being found in many areas, but also because there was a need to know about new murders in case there were any connections with ongoing inquiries elsewhere.

The bodies, which had been discovered over a period of several years, were found in many different circumstances. Some had been dumped into the Green River; others had been left on the riverbank, in ravines, and in quiet country areas; yet others had been covered with loose soil or vegetation. Many individuals had died shortly before they were recovered, whereas others were decomposed or skeletonized, having been discovered many years after they were murdered.

Because the bodies were in varying conditions, with some being incomplete skeletons, the identification process had to be attempted by several different means, such as dental records, fingerprinting, and DNA samples, as well as through the anthropological analysis of bones and medical records.

One of the skeletons was discovered early in 1990 upon a hill.

As the anthropological analysis was conducted, it became apparent that the remains were incomplete, and comprised mainly long bones from the arms and legs, various parts of the torso, and the mandible. Associated with the remains was a medical device. This individual was described as being a young woman in her twenties, of black ancestry, and approximately five feet four inches (1.6 meters) in height.

opposite The Peck Bridge over the Green River, where the first of many victims was found.

right Some of the Green River killer's victims.

below The area known as the Sea-Tac strip associated with the disappearance of many of the victims.

Since the investigators were looking into other cases that may have been connected to the Green River discoveries, their attention was drawn to 1985, when two incomplete human skeletons had been found near Portland, Oregon, close to the border with Washington State. Subsequently, these bodies were identified through information provided from Seattle, and eventually were connected to the Green River investigation. One of the bodies was identified through X-rays taken when the woman involved had undergone surgery to treat a brain condition. The characteristics of the antemortem X-rays produced a positive match with the X-rays taken of the skull during the postmortem examination. This particular medical condition tied in with the medical device found with the remains of the female discovered in the Seattle/ Tacoma area. The characteristics

above Gary Ridgway (2nd L), faces Judge Richard A. Jones after reading a statement at King County Washington Superior Court December 18, 2003.

left Gary Leon Ridgway pleaded guilty to 48 murders dating back more than 20 years.

present in each case were quite compatible, and the skeletal remains were comparatively complete. The body in this case was identified as being one of the victims, who had disappeared after going to buy cigarettes along the "Strip" area of Seattle.

Over the years, the Green River Task Force, with the participation of the FBI, investigated thousands of leads and pieces of evidence. Furthermore, numerous potential suspects had been entered into a database, with the costs

eventually rising to millions of dollars.

However, in early 1987, the authorities came across a strong suspect: Gary Ridgway, had been previously arrested on prostitution charges as far back as 1982 and 1984, and even passed a polygraph test. Although, in 1987, saliva and hair samples had been taken from him, it was not possible to build a strong case against him, at which point the overall investigation ceased.

A breakthrough occurred in 2001 with the advent of more sophisticated technology; DNA samples positively connected Ridgway to some of the victims, and he was subsequently arrested. His wife Judith was oblivious of her husband's activities and had never

heard of the Green River murders as she never took note of the news. When approached by police, she could not comprehend what was happening, as she felt that she had a happy marriage to Gary, who was a kind, loving, and considerate husband. The case went to court and, in 2003, nearly 20 years after the first victims were discovered, Ridgway accepted a guilty plea to 48 charges of first-degree murder, dating from 1982 to 1998, which allowed him to avoid the death penalty; he also confessed to murdering at least 71 women.

From prison he sent Judith scores of letters including poems. She finally filed for divorce and has not had further contact with him. In 2007 a book was published about her life.

Mark S. Putnam

Mark Putnam had a childhood dream of becoming an FBI agent. Eventually, he achieved his goal when he graduated from the FBI Academy in 1987. Putnam was stationed at Pikeville, Kentucky, where he lived with his wife and two children.

In the course of his investigations, Putnam dealt with several informants on a regular basis. One of them was Susan D. Smith. Smith was divorced with two children, and was known to have been a drug user. She often disappeared for long periods of time, and it was believed that she was occasionally involved in prostitution.

Smith enjoyed Putnam's attentions; he showed her a world that she found fascinating and which she saw as a means of escaping from the life she despised. Eventually, they became sexually involved, which ultimately brought an end to his career, his family life, and his ambitions.

By the middle of 1989, Putnam was living in Florida, and Smith confided to some friends that she was pregnant with his child. When he was required to return to Pikeville in June of the same year for a court case, he stayed at the Landmark Hotel, along with other witnesses, including Susan Smith.

Smith took advantage of this situation and confronted Putnam, causing a scene in his room. She became loud and aggressive and, as a result, Putnam suggested that they go for a drive to cool off and

talk in a more rational manner. Eventually, they ended up on a quiet country road. As they sat in the car, Smith became more and more excited, threatening to inform the FBI and Putnam's wife about the pregnancy if he did not agree to arrange a divorce and marry her. The argument became physical when Smith started to slap and scratch him. At some point, Putnam grabbed her by the throat with both hands and held her for a moment. When all went quiet, he released her, but Smith went limp. In desperation, Putnam tried to wake her until he realized that he had killed her.

Overwhelmed by grief and unable to believe his actions, he decided to drive back to the hotel with Smith's body in the trunk of his rental car.

During the next day, Putnam attended to his police business, pretending that nothing had happened. Finally, after driving around with Smith's body in the trunk for nearly a day, he headed out of town until he came to a mine road, located five miles (eight kilometers) from Pikeville. The surrounding area was rarely frequented and there he removed Smith's body from the car and

dragged it through the undergrowth to a ravine, not far from the road. He removed all her clothing, then left the scene.

Eventually, Smith was listed as a missing person, but Putnam was never investigated formally. During the following 12 months, he was plagued with guilt, which caused him to suffer from bouts of diarrhea, insomnia, and compulsive scratching. Eventually, in June 1990, Putnam confessed to the accidental strangling of Smith and informed the authorities where her remains were to be found. Her body was discovered exactly where Putnam had said it would be. Because of the nature of the find, an anthropologist was called in to retrieve the scattered skeletal remains, which had been scavenged. The remains were positively identified through an odontological (dental) analysis.

Putnam received a 16-year sentence upon conviction for first-degree manslaughter. In 1998 and 1999, he appealed for parole, which was denied in both instances. Eventually, in 2000, having served 10 years of his prison sentence in Pennsylvania, Putnam was released.

opposite Former FBI agent Mark Putnam awaits sentencing for the murder of Susan Smith.

The Missing Restaurateur

During the month of April 2000, police officers in the east of England were called to a scene where a human leg had been discovered lying on the ground. Because of the nature of the case, the authorities called in forensic anthropologist Corinne Duhig. Dr. Duhig found a well-preserved lower leg and foot, which had been severed just below the knee. As she continued to search the area, she discovered a shallow pit in which small bones could be seen.

The pit was excavated, resulting in the discovery of a skeletonized lower leg, also severed below the knee, along with a decomposing foot. In addition, there was a section of a black pair of pants that had been made from a high-quality fabric, and a piece of white shirt material was found upon the ground nearby.

After examining the remains, the anthropologist determined that both legs belonged to a short, heavily built male. The missing-persons register suggested that the possible identity of this individual was Mohammed El-Saeedi (fictitious name used). El-Saeedi was a local restaurateur, who had left work one evening in 1999, never to be seen again. His description was compatible in that he was a short and stocky individual. Additional information from the missing-persons register gave his age as mid-twenties, and he was last seen wearing a white shirt and black pants.

DNA was extracted from the remains and compared to the DNA of a close relative. A positive identification was made, but a murder inquiry was not possible, since, in the United Kingdom, a pair of legs does not constitute a body.

In August of the same year, the police in another county were informed that human bones had been discovered beside a main highway. According to the testimony of a child, earlier in the year a "mass of maggots" had been witnessed at the same location. Subsequently, Dr. Duhig located a shallow grave near the site of this latest discovery, and determined, by examining the cuts made in the soil, that it was probable that the digging had been done by two individuals, since the digging pattern was not consistent.

The exhumation produced a semi-skeletonized torso, lacking the arms and the head. Other bone fragments were found in the soil of the grave fill, including the right side of a broken jaw. Additionally, fragments of clothing were discovered, some of them from a black pair of wool pants.

At the scene, Dr. Duhig made an assessment of the remains, which indicated that they were those of a male of heavy build, between 19 and 34 years of age, and about 5 ft 6 in (1.7 m) in height. At the morgue, the arm bones and vertebrae showed evidence of having been cut with a sharp instrument. A DNA test was conducted again, and a positive identification was obtained.

At this point, the police force that had handled the previous case was contacted once again. After comparing both cases, the authorities decided to initiate a murder investigation.

Two acquaintances of El-Saeedi, refered to here as Mr. C. and Mr. H., were proved to have been with him around the time of his disappearance. In a vehicle belonging to Mr. C., traces of blood were discovered, and subsequently digging tools were removed from the homes of both men. It was found that these tools bore soil matching the deposition sites.

During October 2000, another site was investigated as a result of information obtained by the police, and a bone fragment was discovered, as well as a shirt collar. The bone constituted part of the left side of a jaw and matched the section of jaw discovered in August. After forensic examination, the shirt collar was found to bear blood from El-Saeedi and also gunpowder residue.

A trial took place in December 2000, which resulted in Mr. C. being found guilty of murder, whereas Mr. H. was convicted of aiding in the concealment of the body. A motive was never established. It was determined that El-Saeedi had been shot, and that his body had been dismembered and concealed at various locations, which had led to different types and degrees of preservation. The head and hands have never been recovered.

opposite A severed human leg found on the ground.

below left A shallow grave containing human remains.

below A long bone with evidence of cuts.

5 Altered Remains— Hiding Identities

In the forensic field, cases may occur where the characteristics of a corpse have been purposely obliterated to conceal the identity of the victim. The methods utilized to alter human remains vary widely, from dismemberment or burning to using corrosive substances, or a combination of these means. Victims of this type of aggression may not always be unknown to the murderer; in fact, in many instances, the victim is a family member or close friend.

When an inquiry involves the intentional concealment of the victim's identity, it may prove much more difficult for the investigators to solve the case. Nonetheless, forensic science has developed a variety of techniques to assist the positive identification of victims of crimes of this type, their use being dictated by the condition of the remains recovered.

Hiding identity

Throughout history, the human body has been mutilated in a variety of ways, often as a result of rituals or physical punishment. The Aztecs of Mexico practiced human sacrifice on a regular basis, the blood of the individual being offered to the gods as the ultimate gift, since blood represented life. For many, the opportunity of being a sacrificial victim was seen as an honor, and they would offer no resistance. The victim would lie on a stone altar, and a priest would use a stone knife to remove the heart, holding it in his hands while it was still pumping.

During the mid-16th century, other rituals manifested themselves in the guise of hideous punishments. Subjects of the English King Henry VIII who had been convicted of treason would often be sentenced to being hung, drawn, and quartered. The unlucky individual would be hung until near death, then removed from the scaffold. At this point, he or she would be disemboweled while still alive, the genital organs being cut off and burned in the process. Finally, the remains would be cut, or "quartered," and the sections of the body frequently taken to separate parts of the kingdom to be used as visible deterrents against others who may have considered committing acts of treason themselves.

Today, mutilation is committed by murderers for a variety of reasons. These may include the intentional alteration of the victim's identity, brutality during the act of murder or during a state of rage, and necrophilic and cannibalistic practices (see case study No. 9). Various weapons may be used, including machetes, chisels, axes, and electric saws.

Mutilation may be part of the killing process or may be committed after death. The question as to when cuts were made may be answered if tissue is recovered from the area where the injuries were inflicted. A microscopic analysis of the tissue sample will be undertaken by a pathologist, to determine whether the tissue affected by the wounds displayed a vital reaction. This alludes to the soft tissue cells exhibiting a reaction to damage. If this proves to be the case, the cuts will have occurred while the individual was still alive.

« Mutilation is committed by murderers for a variety of reasons. These may include the intentional alteration of the victim's identity, brutality during the act of murder or during a state of rage, and necrophilic and cannibalistic practices. »

above An Aztec human sacrifice. Here the blood of the sacrificial victim is offered to the gods.

When mutilation is designed to conceal the identity of the victim, the facial features are often removed, such as the nose, lips, and ears (see case study No. 19). In other situations, the hands are removed, preventing identification by fingerprint analysis. When the head is removed, not only is the identity concealed, but also, in many cases, the cause of death, if this was due to cranial gunshot wounds or bludgeoning. This may hinder the authorities greatly in their investigation.

The disposal of human remains in cases of foul play can vary from simply being left in a landfill site or a quiet rural area to being burned. In the last case, human remains do not burn completely when exposed to a casual fire, since the temperature produced in such situations is insufficient to consume the soft tissues and the bones. These may be altered in their nature or appearance, but will not turn to ash (see Chapter 7). Even when the soft tissues are altered, they often protect the bones and teeth, which permit accurate identification to be made.

right A victim being hung, drawn, and quartered as a punishment for treason during the 16th century in England.

When a body has not been reduced to ashes, the murderer may, in desperation, try to grind up the remains, as a case from the 1990s illustrates well. The victim was a woman who had been murdered by her husband. He had attempted to burn her body for several hours in an open field. Since the corpse had not turned to ashes, he elected to use heavy equipment to grind up the remains. However, the resulting tiny fragments of bone were collected at the scene. After being subjected to DNA analysis, they provided a positive identification and an eventual murder conviction.

Other cases may involve the use of powerful corrosive substances. Many of these, especially the alkaline types, are found in products that we use every day. However, because their concentration is small in household products, as a general rule they cause no harm. When considering how to dispose of a body, some criminals elect to place the victim's remains in a container with a caustic substance, intending to dissolve the body (see case study No. 4), thereby disposing of evidence that can link them to the crime. Among such substances, which cause damage to soft tissue, bone, teeth, nails, and hair are phosphoric, sulfuric, and hydrochloric acid.

above left Alphonse Bertillon (1853–1914).

above right Cesare Lombroso (1835–1909) suggested that criminal traits could be identified through facial characteristics.

Corrosives can be divided into acids and bases, the acids being recognizable by their chemical formulae, because they always have the prefix letter "H." For example, sulfuric acid has the chemical formula H_2SO_4 and is used commercially in car batteries, and in the process of refining gasoline. This particular acid is so powerful that it can burn a hole through a piece of iron. Another dangerous acid is hydrochloric acid (HCl), which actually occurs in the stomachs of humans as a constituent of the digestive fluids. However, the stomach lining produces a mucus to protect itself from such strong acids; if it does not, problems may result, such as peptic ulcers.

The bases, which are referred to as alkalines, are recognizable because their chemical formulae will always include the letters "OH"—for example, sodium hydroxide's formula is NaOH. Also known as caustic soda or lye, sodium hydroxide is utilized in the production of soaps and other cleaning materials. Potassium hydroxide (KOH), popularly known as caustic potash, is also used in the production of soap.

In the forensic context, the chemical reactions produced by corrosive substances damage a body by eating away the soft and hard tissues. There have been circumstances in which human remains have been exposed to such corrosives in the hope that their identities would be obliterated as a result of the remains dissolving over time. Depending on the amount of exposure and the type of substance used, the damage caused to a body will vary. Substances such as hydrochloric acid can dissolve a body within hours, sometimes in a 20-hour span; the power of these substances allows even the tiniest amount introduced to the facial region to cause considerable alteration to the bones and teeth.

Other damage to the body is caused by blunt instruments, or by the impact of large-caliber bullets in the facial and cranial areas, which may distort the characteristics of the victim. In such instances, the forensic anthropologist can reconstruct the damaged area, returning it to a state that allows reconstruction or reproduction of the victim's facial characteristics to be possible.

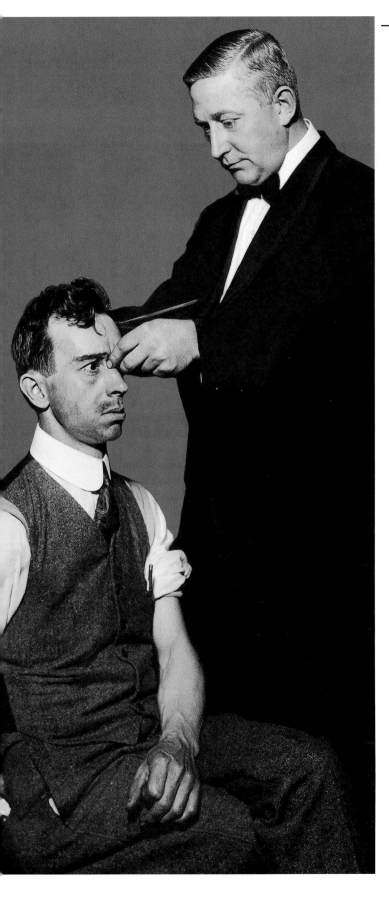

left In the late 19th century, Alphonse Bertillon put into practice his system of criminal identification, which comprised photographing the subject looking directly at the camera, then in profile, with the camera centered on the right ear. The subject's height, along with the length of a foot, an arm, and an index finger, would also be recorded.

Facial reconstruction and reproduction

As forensic science progresses technologically, new techniques are constantly being developed to assist in establishing the identities of the deceased. Originally, not all the techniques used were intended to identify victims of crime. Instead, they were created in an attempt to identify and apprehend criminals. In the 1800s, the reproduction of facial characteristics was a revolutionary concept, since up to that time, the oral testimony of witnesses to the crime was the only source of information available to the authorities.

During the latter half of the 1800s, an Italian medical doctor, Cesare Lombroso, claimed that after studying the facial characteristics of thousands of criminals, he could identify specific individuals who possessed criminal traits. He also claimed he could determine the type of criminal activity in which they would engage. For obvious reasons, his methods were flawed and, as a result, many innocent individuals were labeled as criminals.

Also interested in using facial characteristics to identify criminals was the Frenchman Alfonse Bertillon. He was the first to propose systematic methods that supposedly would "identify" prospective criminals. Bertillon's method involved measuring the head and face of a criminal at

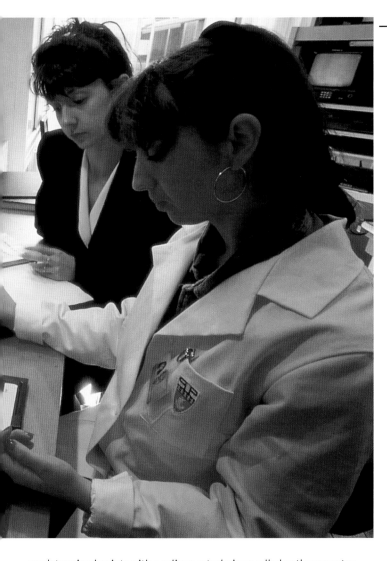

left A researcher helping a victim of crime to compose an image of a criminal's face using the Identikit method.

predetermined points with a caliper, a technique called anthropometry, which translates as "the measurement of man." The measurements were recorded and filed and, if the same individual reoffended, identification would be possible by comparing the measurements taken upon their arrest with those on record. This method was adopted by the French, as well as the authorities in other European countries and the United States. However, it had its pitfalls, since not all personnel took the prescribed measurements in exactly the same manner. This meant that, occasionally, innocent individuals, who possessed similar characteristics to known criminals, would be arrested, falsely accused, and even wrongly convicted.

Another method of identification introduced by Bertillon was known as portrait parlé (speaking likeness). This method involved compiling the physical description of a criminal by having a witness select a series of characteristics from an existing list. Eventually, this concept evolved into what is now known as the Identikit, introduced in the 1940s by the American Hugh McDonald. His system consisted of a series of transparencies, each showing a different facial characteristic. These could be superimposed on each another to create a composite portrait, based upon eyewitness testimony. Over the years, this method has proved of great value in securing the identification and arrest of many criminals.

Toward the end of the 1800s and beginning of the 1900s, an interest developed in the use of facial features to assist in the identification of crime victims instead of the perpetrators. One pioneer was Wilhelm His, who, in 1895, tried to reconstruct the facial characteristics of the composer Johann Sebastian Bach directly from the skull, using clay for the sculpture. His reconstruction was based upon studies that he had made of the thickness of facial soft tissue on several cadavers. His had proved that the thickness is remarkably constant between one individual and another, the main difference being the facial contours. He compiled a table of specific tissue thickness for various facial landmarks, which even today is being modified to encompass modern populations, although the basic concept is followed for every facial reproduction.

For the forensic anthropologist, these new techniques, which have become further refined through the use of computer technology, are of great assistance and significance. This is because many cases received by anthropological laboratories require special means of identification beyond simple manual examination. Among the new technologies available is multislice computer tomography scanning (MSCT), whereby the digital images produced during a postmortem examination will allow the forensic anthropologist specialized in this field, or a forensic artist, to conduct a series of osteometric analyses (bone measurements) to determine the individual's particular facial traits, thereby producing an image which will aid in a visual identification of the remains.

The facial reconstruction of a skull may be required for a variety of reasons—for example, as a result of fragmentation caused by the use of a blunt instrument, the impact of a large-caliber bullet, or an explosion. The forensic anthropologist is responsible for reconstructing recovered bone fragments and assembling them by using his or her knowledge of bone anatomy. Such bone fragments are held together with the aid of different types of glue. Based on the results, the characteristics of the individual are assessed, such as sex, ancestry, and any particular features, such as facial asymmetry. The last is the phenomenon by which one side of an individual's face, or certain features, may be of a noticeably different size

right An anthropologist reconstructing a skull.

opposite A three-dimensional model made for police identification purposes in Manchester, England.

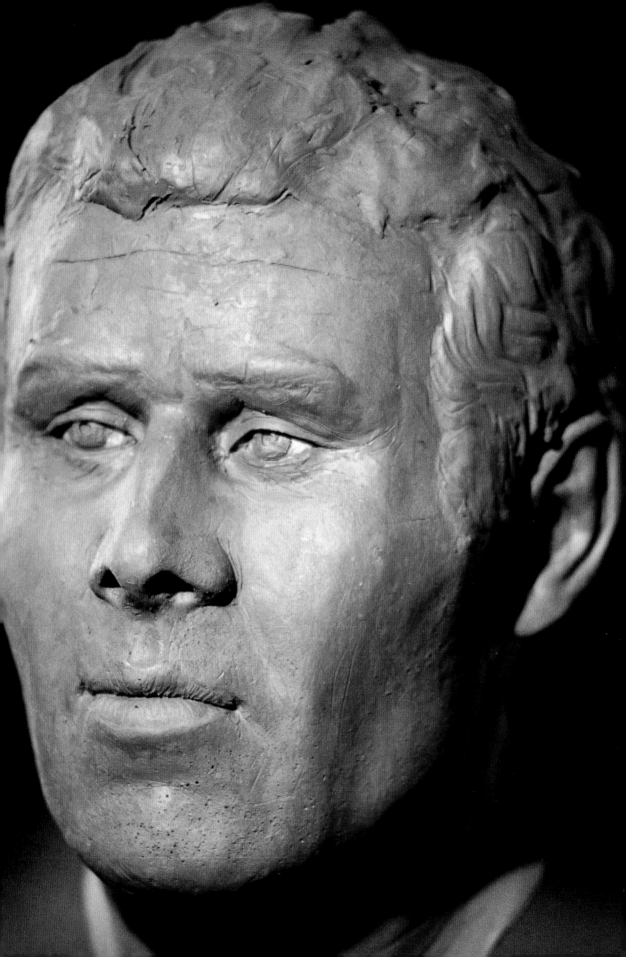

to the other. When unusual facial characteristics are present, such as in the area of the chin, cheekbones, or forehead, a more accurate reproduction may result from the analysis made.

On occasion, a virtually complete skull may be discovered, but it may exhibit minor alterations due to the use of caustic substances or burning. In this situation, a facial reproduction of the characteristics present may be attempted without any modifications being made to the bones. In any case, a reproduction can be achieved by several means, depending upon the field of expertise of the artist, as well as the resources available to the investigators. However, regardless of the type of reproduction chosen, the anthropologist and the artist work together to produce the final result.

Three-dimensional technique

The three-dimensional reproduction of facial features that His pioneered in the late 1800s is widely used to recreate the features of individuals from skulls recovered from archeological sites. When the need arises, artists who employ this technique are called upon to aid forensic investigations. These artists possess an excellent understanding of facial anatomy, and are able to reproduce and position the facial muscles accurately according to the characteristics of the skull. To begin, the artist places a series of tissue markers upon specific landmarks of the face. These markers vary in size to indicate the different depths and quantities of clay required on various zones of the face, which may also be influenced by the sex, age, and ancestry of the individual. The clay is gradually molded onto the face, using the markers as guides. A wig and artificial eyes are usually added when the modeling of the face is complete, to make the final result more lifelike.

Nowadays, revolutionary computer software allows three-dimensional reproductions to be completed. Computers also speed up the process of reconstruction and allow alterations to be made with greater ease, as well as being more cost-effective. In general, the choice of a manual or computerized technique depends upon the preference of those involved in the task.

Sketches and video-superimposition

When handmade sketches are used to re-create facial features, the first task is to produce a life-size photograph of the skull. Then a composite artist will draw the facial features over the photograph, using special paper. As with the three-dimensional clay technique, markers are employed to indicate the thickness of the facial tissue. However, modern software makes it possible for forensic scientists to utilize computers to do the drawing. The image of the skull is generated on the screen, and the artist "draws" over it by giving commands to the computer. The advantage offered by this technique, compared to hand-drawn sketches, is that it provides the opportunity of adding or deleting facial features with ease. The blending of different features is possible too, such as the hairline with the skin of the forehead. Other options include the ability to change the color of the eyes, and also to adjust the hairstyle with relatively little effort. Additionally, such programs provide the opportunity of removing part of the "sketch" to make comparisons with different features of the skull, or to superimpose the different images so that they can be viewed and compared simultaneously.

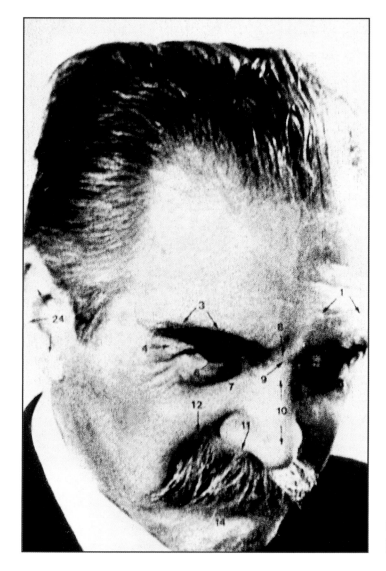

left Facial landmarks observed on Josef Mengele's face to aid in his identification.

Video-superimposition, on the other hand, is used when the investigators possess an existing picture of the potential victim, allowing it to be superimposed directly onto the skull. One of the first cases in which this technique was employed was to identify a murder victim in Scotland in the early 20th century (see case study No. 19). In this case, the contours of a mutilated skull were matched with those contained in a photograph of the deceased. With the aid of modern computer software designed specifically for this purpose, a skull may be projected onto the screen, together with a scan produced from a photograph. The two images can then be superimposed, and the main facial landmarks and tissue thickness compared.

Another example of the application of this particular technique is the case of Josef Mengele, better known as the "Angel of Death." Mengele performed experiments upon Jews detained in concentration camps during World War II. After the war, he disappeared, but 40 years later, in 1985, his remains were discovered in Brazil, although his skull had been extensively

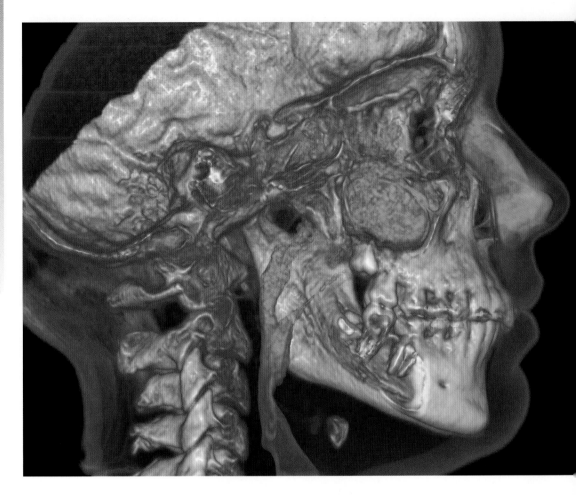

above Cone beam CT scanners produce fast results and the images can be converted by a computer into a three-dimensional model.

fragmented as a result of a clumsy exhumation. Dr. Clyde Snow, the anthropologist assigned to the task of identifying the remains, reassembled the skull fragments, and subsequently these were compared with an old photograph of Mengele. By utilizing skull and photograph video-superimposition, Dr. Snow felt that a positive match had been made. When other evidence was also considered, the skull was finally deemed to be that of Mengele.

With the use of computed tomography 3D image (3D-CT image) a skull can be compared with a photograph of the alleged victim taken in life. This allows to compare soft tissue thickness and the alignment of anatomical points, thereby assessing its degree of compatibility. An additional and similar method involves using computer software which permits the user to wipe away or fade in sections of the reference image in order to assess compatibility.

Because CT images permit the reconstruction of bone, this technique can be used in cases when the remains are burned, mummified, or decomposed in order to carry out a comparison. In the past, this process would have involved the maceration of soft tissues in order to access the bones, an extremely time-consuming process; the new procedure saves valuable time for those involved, with the identification being confirmed in a more timely manner.

Cone beam CT images, as used by dentists within clinical practice, allow a detailed analysis of the dental structures, diseases, and decay to be assessed, important for forensic odontologists when compiling a positive identification.

The procedures and techniques used in facial reproduction are valuable tools in the task of identifying the remains of individuals. When the results are added to other skeletal, dental, and DNA analyses, they contribute to a final positive identification.

The same electronic imaging programs are also used to show the effects of the maturing and aging process on missing children and criminals on the run. This has resulted in considerable success in locating individuals.

A final, but interesting, point is that now forensic anthropologists are able to participate in identifying criminals, too. Aided by computer technologies, they may be asked to help identify criminals caught on CCTV cameras located in banks and other business establishments where crimes have taken place. Not only can images be obtained at the time of the crime, but in some cases, CCTV cameras provide footage at a time before or after the event. In such instances, a computer may be used to compare still and moving images of the perpetrator with those of the suspect.

Once the suspect is in custody, photographs are taken at similar angles from those obtained from CCTV footage. Furthermore, a video is also

above Portable high-resolution CT scanner, which fires beams of X-rays (left) at different angles around the skull. The X-rays are detected on an imaging plate (right) and the data converted by computer into a three-dimensional model.

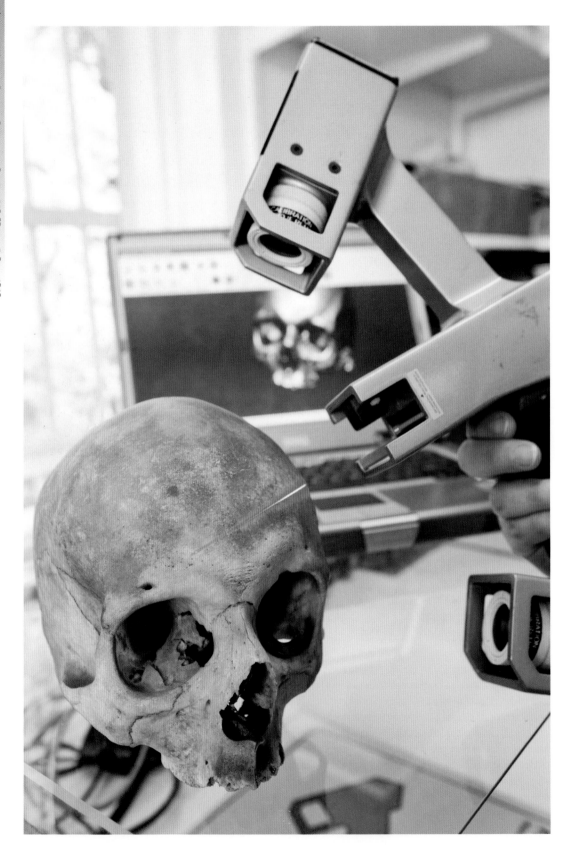

produced in order to match movement and specific mannerisms. This often leads to a positive result and eventually to a successful conviction.

In order to complete the required comparisons, the forensic anthropologist will receive both sets of data; among the characteristics sought when comparing still images are facial features, individual characteristics in proportionality, and overall head shape. With specific reference to video footage, gait and specifics in mannerisms are of the utmost importance; individuals possess particularities with respect to their movements that may be extremely subtle, and possibly unnoticed by the person themselves, or others close to him or her. Among such elements are the stride, positioning of the feet when walking, the angle at which the head is held, and arm movements, in addition to the height of the individual with reference to different points upon the body. However, under the scrutiny of a trained professional, such aspects of body movement and mannerisms are key points for a proper identification.

The technique used is called photogrammetry, and it allows measurements to be taken from a photograph; although this technique is not recent, in combination with computer software it allows new advantages with respect to identification process. As such, photographs from different angles and in sequence can be perceived by the software and a virtual three-dimensional image produced. Landmarks selected as points of reference for the identification process are chosen by the specialists dependent upon the observations made; the results can then be portrayed as line images with accurate measurements between landmarks.

above Security cameras mounted in a high position. The images captured can be used by forensic anthropologists when identifying an alleged suspect.

opposite Modern technology is utilized for digital facial reconstruction. It combines anatomical reconstruction with soft tissue thickness guides.

This correlation process does not entail positive identification but is of great use when no conclusive findings are available; the authorities may then decide if and when DNA analysis or fingerprinting is required.

Forensic image analysis can also aid in assessing static height of a particular individual by comparing it to height indicated during movement as captured through surveillance cameras.

Problems encountered with this technology may involve variables such as crowded areas of population, such as busy stores or streets, and also physical obstructions within the video image. Perpetrators who are disguised may not be readily identifiable, but their characteristics of motion can be more comprehensively analyzed.

Other cases have involved the use of computer software to compare two pictures, thought to be of the same individual, when his or her identity has been brought into question. One limitation of this technique is that both pictures must be taken from the same angle and distance. In countries where there is a national registry, pictures taken of the population are of a regular pattern, which helps greatly if identification is required by this method.

right Processing of CCTV images may result in 3D representations that are highly precise in terms of measurements (segment length, stature, etc.) and enable gait analysis. *Lynnerup N, Vedel J, 2005. Person Identification by Gait Analysis and Photogrammetry.* Journal of Forensic Sciences, 50(1): 112-118.

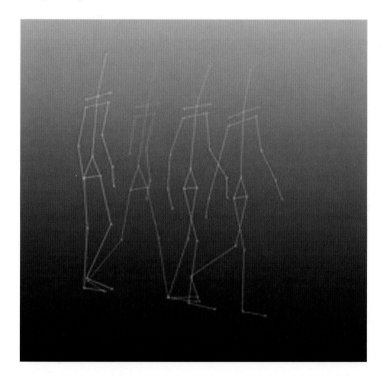

By using such techniques, anthropologists are now working with the living as well as the dead, and also are becoming a greater factor in the successful apprehension of criminals by law enforcement agencies around the world.

Tattoos
The normal method of creating a tattoo involves injecting ink into the skin. However, tattoos may also be produced more simply by inserting a needle wrapped with ink-soaked thread into the skin, whereas others may be

formed by electronic devices. Tattooing has been practiced by a variety of cultures throughout history, and many meanings have been attributed to tattoos—for example, they have been used as a quick means of identifying prisoners. In the case of Western societies, tattoos have been traditionally popular with certain sectors of the population, such as prison inmates, bikers, and members of the military. They may also be used to identify an individual as a member of a specific organization, as was the case with the Waffen SS in Germany during the Nazi era.

Tattoos can often serve as excellent means of identification. Therefore, it is vital for forensic personnel to be able to identify, photograph, and record them as part of the postmortem analysis. Once a body begins to decompose, the colors within a tattoo will start to lose their intensity and fade, until the tattoo may no longer be visible. Unless certain techniques are used, tattoos may not be seen, and their possible value in aiding identification will be lost.

When a tattoo is thought to be present, but decomposition has obliterated it from view, the area is rubbed with a solution of hydrogen peroxide. This causes the tattoo to be "highlighted" against the darkening

below Tattoos are created by injecting ink under the skin.

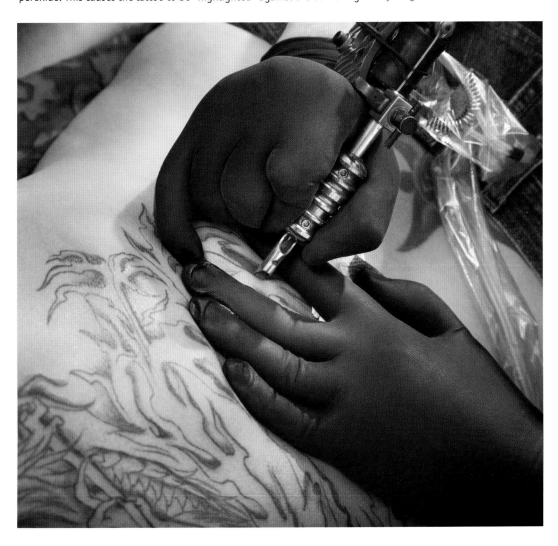

of the skin caused by decomposition. The tattoo will remain visible for several hours, before gradually fading away again. Another method used to locate faded tattoos is to employ alternative light sources. When such lights are shone on the suspected area, they will cause certain types of ink to be illuminated.

Imaging and internal structures

Radiographs and computer tomography scanned images are used by physicians to interpret internal maladies and fractures. Yet, in the forensic field, such internal structures can be excellent means of identification; individual bones, such as the long bones in the extremities, may differ from one person to another with respect to their volume and structure. Additionally, the shape of the bones—for example, the vertebrae of the spinal column and pelvic bones—may display minute variations in morphology which can be noted by the trained eye.

Another area of interest for radiographic analysis is the frontal sinus. The human body has cavities called sinuses, found within tissues such as bones. Those in the skull are called paranasal sinuses, and they act as drainage openings into the nasal cavity. These sinuses can cause severe pain when infected, as is sometimes the case when a person has a cold. One of these paranasal sinuses, the frontal sinus, is located above the nose, inside the forehead. The shape of it is unique to each individual, allowing its use as a means of positive identification, provided that an antemortem X-ray can be located to compare with one taken during the postmortem examination. This particular method is used in cases where the facial and cranial regions of the skull have been severely fragmented.

opposite Left foreleg and ankle showing an old fracture that healed incorrectly. The fibula bows outward due to the extra bone growth on the tibia.

right Colored X-ray image of a person's skull seen from the front. The orange and purple areas highlight the paranasal sinuses—the shape of the frontal sinuses are unique to the individual.

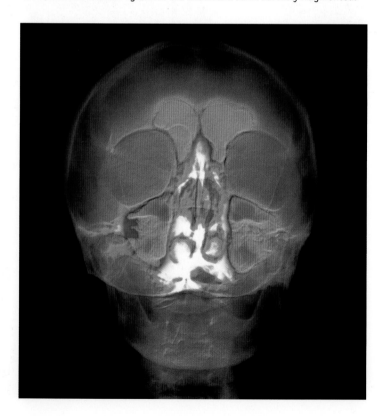

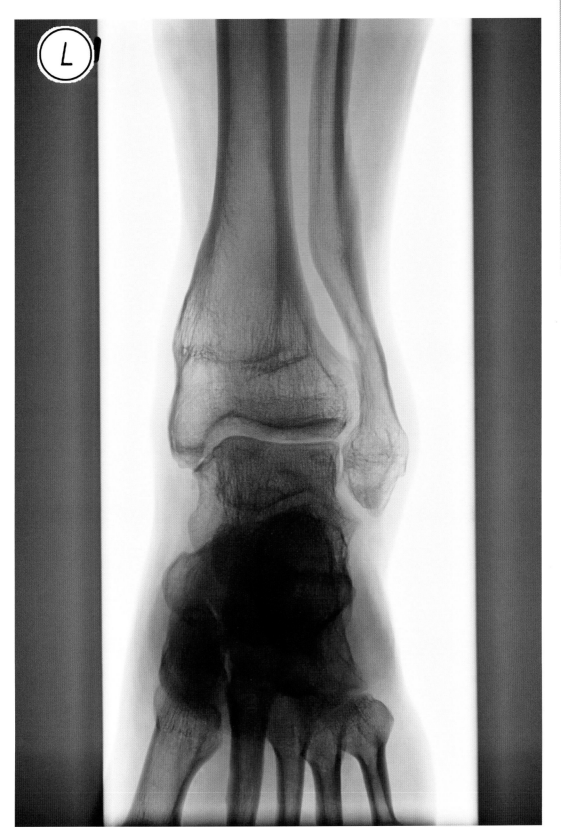

Buck Walker

In May 1974, Eleanor Graham, better known to her friends and family as Muff, and her husband, Malcolm, left San Diego on their expensive sailboat, the Sea Wind, on a journey toward Hawaii. Nearly two weeks later, they arrived at Big Island, where they stocked up with food supplies and other items necessary for their long journey and stay in the South Pacific.

The Grahams were headed for an atoll called Palmyra, in search of adventure and paradise. Palmyra Atoll is under US jurisdiction and constitutes one of the last uninhabited places in the world, complete with palm trees, coral reefs, lagoons, and thick vegetation. It is also dotted with the remains of abandoned buildings, equipment, and a runway that had been used by the US Navy when the atoll was a military post during World War II.

The Grahams reached Palmyra a month later and, to their surprise, they discovered that another couple had arrived a week earlier. The couple introduced themselves as Roy Allen and Jennifer Jenkins. Unknown to the Grahams, however, Allen's real name was Buck Walker, and he was running from the law on drug charges.

Walker and Jenkins were traveling on the Iola, a vessel that was not very seaworthy, and had a very limited supply of food with them. They told the Grahams that they planned to live off the land by growing vegetables and fishing.

Various people visited the island while the two couples were there, among them Bob Wolfe and Norman Sanders of Oregon. They were also touring the Pacific and had decided to stop at the island for a few days. They departed on August 17, leaving the two couples alone again.

As a general rule, each Wednesday, Malcolm spoke to a friend, Curt Shoemaker in Hawaii, using a two-way radio. On the first Wednesday of September, Shoemaker called the Grahams, but there was no reply. He tried again a week later, but to no avail. Alarmed, he contacted the Coast Guard, but they elected not to search the area on the grounds that failure to communicate by radio was not a reason to believe that the couple had gone missing.

The weeks went by, and in October of the same year, the Sea

right Malcolm Graham and his wife "Muff" aboard their sailboat, the Sea Wind.

opposite Buck Walker in court. He was sentenced to life imprisonment in 1985 for the murder of Eleanor Graham.

radiographs and records held by her dentist in San Diego.

According to the odontologist, the jawbone and the teeth had been severely fractured, indicating that the damage had probably been caused by a blunt object. Additionally, the pathologists reported that the long bones had suffered complete fractures, which can only occur if the body is put under extreme stress. However, the bones failed to produce indications of the cause of death.

When the analysis was given to the investigating anthropologist, Dr. D. Ubelaker, he noted a white irregular marking along the top of the skull. Upon close inspection, he realized that the area was calcinated. The pattern it exhibited led him to conclude that this had been caused by intense heat applied to the head while soft tissue was still present. He believed that this had occurred upon Mrs. Graham's death, or very soon after she had died, but how it was inflicted upon her was not possible to determine.

Buck Walker and Jennifer Jenkins were charged separately with the murder of Eleanor Graham. Walker was sentenced to life imprisonment in 1985, and his sentence was ordered to run concurrently with time to be served from his prior convictions. This ensured that he could not apply for parole for at least 21 years. Jenkins was found innocent of all charges. Malcolm Graham's body was still missing at the time of the trial and has not been recovered since.

Walker was granted parole and was released from prison in 2007. He settled near San Francisco, and died three years later at the age of 72. He maintained his innocence to the end.

Wind arrived in Hawaii with Walker and Jenkins on board. The boat had been repainted, and Walker told several people that he had won it gambling. However, someone did recognize the sailboat and raised the alarm. Both Walker and Jenkins were arrested and eventually tried for theft.

Six years later, Robert and Sharon Jordan arrived at Palmyra. One day, as Sharon Jordan was walking along the beach, she noticed something glittering nearby. She realized that the object was the gold crown of a tooth.

Subsequently, the Jordans also found a human skull, some arm and leg bones, and an aluminum container that held a piece of cloth, a bone, and a wristwatch. They informed the authorities in Hawaii, and suspicions were aroused that the discoveries might be connected to the missing couple. Eventually, the FBI became involved, but they could not locate further remains.

The bones were sent for forensic analysis and were identified as belonging to Eleanor Graham. Positive identification was made by comparing her teeth with

James S. Vlassakis

In 1994, a farmer in Lower Light, north of Adelaide, South Australia, came across some skeletal remains. But the nature of this discovery did not become significant until 1999, when more bodies were discovered in unusual circumstances. This case would develop many twists and turns.

The latest discoveries came from Snowtown, a small rural farming community with a population of slightly over 500 people, also situated to the north of Adelaide.

The police, concerned about several people who had been reported missing in the area since 1993, formed an extensive task force. A long and detailed investigation led them to a brick building that once had housed a branch of the State Bank of South Australia. In the old vault, to their disbelief, they discovered six black plastic barrels containing human body parts submerged in acid, including 15 human feet.

The investigators continued gathering evidence, which resulted in the arrest of three men, who lived in different areas of Adelaide, the state capital of Southern Australia. All three were charged with murder. Some days later, a fourth man, James S. Vlassakis, was arrested.

As the investigation continued, still more bodies were discovered.

The police searched the former house of one of the accused, in the belief that more bodies might be recovered. They removed concrete that had been laid over the suspected burial area and proceeded to search with ground-penetrating radar. This portable instrument will indicate in minutes if there are disturbances in the soil, and in this particular case, it proved positive. The investigating team initiated a careful excavation, which exposed a body about 6 ft (1.8 meters) below the ground that had been stuffed into two separate bags. Because an analysis of the excavated area had been made, the forensic team realized that there was yet another disturbance beneath the body that had been

opposite The farmhouse associated with the Snowtown murders.

right A forensic officer carries out bags containing small bones.

below Grave site where two bodies were found in barrels.

above One of the men arrested in connection with the murder of ten people in South Australia.

right James Vlassakis leaves the Supreme Court after pleading guilty.

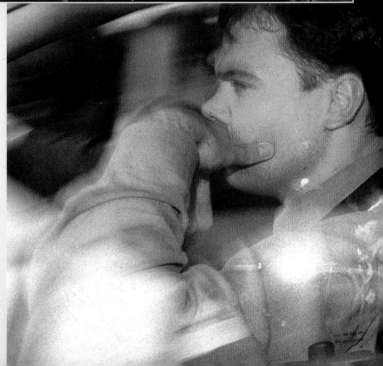

exhumed, resulting in the discovery of another body. So far, the police had discovered a total of 11 bodies.

The forensic identification of the victims was conducted using a multidisciplinary approach. The scientists were able to obtain DNA and matched it with those of the living relatives of some of the victims. Others were identified through fingerprint analysis. Anthropologists were also able to match a radiograph with characteristics noted upon the human remains originally discovered in 1994 at Lower Light.

According to forensic psychiatry, if serial killings are carried out by a group of individuals, the most likely motive will be financial gain. Such was the motive in this particular case, and the victims were all known by, or related to, the killers. Vlassakis murdered both his stepbrother and a half-brother, who were identified eventually as being two of the individuals found in the barrels of acid.

By killing these people, the murderers were able to obtain social security benefit checks that some of them were receiving, as these were sent out on a regular basis, even after some of them had been reported missing.

In June 2001, James S. Vlassakis confessed to the murders of four individuals and was sentenced to life imprisonment. He is eligible for parole in 2025. The remaining three accomplices were also found guilty and sentenced to lengthy terms.

Blake and Davis

Many journalists disappear and are killed when traveling to different regions of the world to cover news stories. Such was the case of Nick Blake, an American journalist, and Griffin Davis, a British photographer, who were 27 and 38 years of age respectively at the times of their deaths.

In 1985, Blake and Davis traveled to Guatemala to investigate the plight of the Mayan communities. After arriving in Guatemala, they journeyed to its northern region, within the Cordillera of Cuchumatanes. This is an area of difficult terrain, due to its steep topography, and it is covered with thick rainforest.

The pair traveled for several days, passing through various peasant communities en route. At some point on their journey, they disappeared, never to arrive at their planned destination. Eventually, friends reported them missing.

Some years later, Blake's brothers asked an individual in Guatemala to investigate the circumstances leading to the disappearance of the men. According to the investigation, they were being escorted by a Civilian Patrol, but had eventually been shot. Their bodies had been left nearby and covered with wood, while their personal effects and working equipment were removed. Several years later, the bodies were exhumed and the bones set alight.

During the early 1990s, thanks to Blake's brothers' insistence and determination, the remains of both bodies were returned to the United

States and were sent to the Smithsonian Institution in Washington, D.C., for analysis.

The physical anthropologist's analysis indicated that the remains were calcinated, and that there were over 1,500 pieces. Because there was duplication of bones, it was determined that the remains represented two individuals. But more data was needed to achieve positive identifications.

Anthropologists from the Smithsonian traveled to Guatemala to visit the site where the bones had been burned and later collected. Using their knowledge of archeological techniques, and by

opposite Rugged terrain typical of the Guatemalan countryside.

above Nick Blake in the mountains of Guatemala, a few weeks before his disappearance.

working in a meticulous manner, they were able to recover more human remains, including teeth, that would help in the identification of the bodies. Additionally, several personal items that pointed to the identity of the victims were also retrieved.

Upon their return to Washington, the scientists analyzed their new skeletal finds, and even though many fragments had been burned, they proved invaluable in the identification of the bodies.

Davis had had some X-rays taken of his frontal sinus some years prior to his death. By comparing these antemortem X-rays with X-rays taken of the

recovered skeletal remains, the scientists were able to prove conclusively that they had identified the remains of Davis. As for Blake, the antemortem dental records were compared with X-rays taken from the recovered teeth, and the characteristics in both provided a positive match.

Even though many years had passed since the killings, and the bodies had been burned and were highly fragmented, the anthropologists investigating this case were able to obtain a positive identification of the remains. As a result, they could be handed over to the victims' families to be laid to rest and provide a sense of closure for their relatives.

Dr. Buck Ruxton

Sometimes murderers think that by dismembering and disfiguring a corpse, the victim's identity will never be discovered. Such was the case of Dr. Buck Ruxton in 1935.

left Dr. Buck Ruxton, hanged in 1936 for the murder of his partner and maid.

below Happier times: Dr. Ruxton with Isabella and one of their children.

opposite left Police searching for remains in a ravine in Moffat, Scotland.

opposite right A picture of Mrs. Ruxton's skull superimposed on her photograph. This method allowed for a positive identification to be made.

Dr. Ruxton, whose real name was Bukhtyar Rustomji Ratanji Hakim, was a physician, originally from India. He lived with Isabella Van Ess, and although they never married, Isabella liked to be called Mrs. Ruxton.

The Ruxtons settled in Lancaster, England, at the beginning of the 1930s, and were known for having a stormy relationship. Dr. Ruxton believed that Isabella was having relationships with other men, and soon his jealousy escalated to physical abuse. On many occasions, Isabella asked for police protection.

In September 1935, the couple had yet another argument sparked by Dr. Ruxton's accusation that his wife was being unfaithful to him. This would prove to be their last confrontation.

Mrs. Ruxton was last seen upon her return from a visit to the English coastal town of Blackpool. However, not only did she go missing, but so did the Ruxton's maid, Mary Rogerson. When questioned, Dr. Ruxton stated that Mrs. Ruxton had decided to take a vacation, and since she was away, he had asked the maid not to come by and take care of the house until Mrs. Ruxton returned.

Nonetheless, he did hire several cleaners to "tidy" his home. All complained of a foul smell inside the house, and of unidentifiable stains and fluids on some of the carpets and in the bathtub.

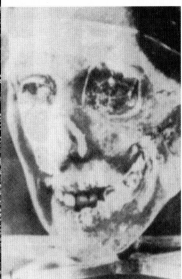

skulls. Positive identification of Mrs. Ruxton was possible, even though the prominent nose and teeth that characterized her had been removed.

Due to the dismemberment of the bodies, the causes of death proved difficult to ascertain. However, after the postmortem had been completed, it was deemed likely that Mrs. Ruxton had been strangled, since the hyoid bone in her throat was fractured. It was surmised that the maid had been asphyxiated, and shortly after the murders both had been dismembered in the bathtub.

Because the newspaper used to wrap some of the remains was a special edition of the Sunday Graphic, which was sold only in the Lancaster area, the murder was connected to Dr. Ruxton. Prompted by the statements of the cleaners about the bloodstains and foul odors in the doctor's home, the police carried out a search of the building, and the evidence they found was used to try him for the murder of both women. He was sentenced to death and hanged at Strangeways Prison, Manchester, in the spring of 1936.

In the meantime, a woman by the name of Mary Johnson had spotted a human arm while taking a stroll by the River Annon, near Moffat, Scotland. The police were notified, and the ensuing search resulted in the recovery of 70 body parts that had been scattered near the river and along the highway between Edinburgh and Carlisle. Some of the remains, which were of two bodies, were wrapped in pages from the Sunday Graphic newspaper, and others were found concealed in clothing.

The human remains had been totally mutilated, some being only remnants of skin. The facial regions were devoid of lips, noses, ears, eyes, and skin. The fingers had been cut into small pieces, and identifying scars had been removed. It was evident that the killer had set out to erase the identity of the two corpses completely.

However, despite the level of damage to the remains, identification of the bodies was still possible, using different means. One of the methods at the disposal of the police was fingerprinting. Although the bodies were badly damaged, the fingerprint areas on some of the digits were still present, allowing positive identification of the maid. Additionally, one of the feet presented a noticeable lateral deviation of the big toe, which was consistent with a condition that she was known to have had.

Another method utilized was the superimposition of a photograph and skull at the Glasgow Medical School, in Scotland. A picture of Mrs. Ruxton was compared with the two mutilated skulls, and by carefully observing the anatomical landmarks of the bones, it was possible to match the picture with one of the

6 Air Disasters

« Every item discovered [at the scene] is flagged to indicate its location, regardless of how small or fragmented it may be, since the association of artifacts with human remains may aid identification as the scene is gradually reconstructed. »

Although air disasters are few and far between, they tend to be remembered for a long time, not least for their devastating effects. When such large-scale accidents occur, the rescue operation must be undertaken with immediate effect in the hope of saving as many lives as possible.

One of the first major civil air disasters occurred in May 1937, when the airship Hindenburg suddenly caught fire while attempting to land in New York, killing 35 people. This German zeppelin was one of the largest aircraft of its time, and it had been transformed into a luxurious flying hotel.

Since then, commercial aviation has evolved rapidly. Today, air travel is considered to be the safest means of mass transportation. It is estimated that only one in seven million people will face hazards while flying, and statistics indicate that the level of safety in relation to the number of accidents has not changed markedly over the years. However, perhaps due to media coverage and the huge increase in flights and passengers taking off daily around the world, the current impression is that safety is not quite as good as it once was.

Air crashes involving large aircraft capable of carrying hundreds of people fall into the category of mass fatal incidents, which may be defined as a situation in which a great deal of destruction has occurred, and in which emergency personnel will need to apply specific techniques for the rescue and treatment of survivors. In addition to airplane crashes, mass disasters include such natural events as earthquakes and floods, sunken ferries, and work-related catastrophes involving explosives or mining.

The steps taken by emergency personnel upon arrival at the scene of a disaster are dictated by the enormity of the situation. Because a large

number of victims is involved, an assessment of what needs to be done must be prioritized, with a triage system being implemented by those in charge of the scene.

A triage is a system of priorities based upon the urgency of the situation encountered. Qualified personnel will assess the condition of the victims, depending upon the severity of the injuries sustained. Decisions can then be made as to which individuals need emergency attention first. In some cases, the victims will be transported by air to nearby hospital emergency rooms. More severe cases may need to be treated immediately at the scene, such as when emergency amputations are required.

Because a triage has to be implemented with extreme care, adequate communications and equipment for the rescue and transportation of the victims are all important in a disaster response. They will allow those qualified to deal with the survivors to work more effectively to save as many lives as possible. The process may be difficult, due to the magnitude of the situation, and because survivors and deceased may be trapped among the debris. Consideration must be given to the facts that such events are usually entirely unanticipated, and that work must be completed quickly, yet in a very organized manner, for a triage to be successful.

Types of accident

Despite advanced technology and the use of computers, airplane accidents may occur for a number of reasons, at any time between takeoff and landing. The cause may be mechanical, such as an engine malfunction, or

opposite The Hindenburg airship bursts into flames while attempting to land in New York.

above Lightning can be a major cause of aircraft accidents.

above A Boeing 747 can carry over 300 passengers.

weather related, such as instances of turbulence, lightning strike, or wind shear. Human error may also play a role, both in and outside the cockpit, or there may be a combination of factors that cause a disaster. An example would be the accident involving two Boeing 747 aircraft at Tenerife Airport in the Canary Islands, in 1977. Both planes were preparing for takeoff, from the same runway, while the airport was shrouded in dense fog. Despite being in radio communication with the tower, one of the pilots decided to takeoff before being given clearance, while the other aircraft was using the same runway to access a taxiway. The resulting collision killed almost 600 people. Runway incursions do not always involve only large aircraft. In Florida, during 2000, four people died when two Cessna airplanes collided while attempting to takeoff at the same time.

When an accident occurs at an airport, during takeoff or landing, emergency personnel are usually close at hand. Airports are equipped with their own highly trained firefighters and paramedics, who will usually arrive at the scene moments after the incident occurs. Their function is not only to put out any fire, but also to provide a means of escape for passengers if the normal exits are unusable, as is often the case. Yet, even when the target of reaching an accident within three minutes is accomplished, casualties may result from the inhalation of toxic fumes or the presence of superheated air. Such conditions usually occur after a crash because commercial airliners customarily carry thousands of gallons of fuel, especially when embarking on long-haul flights.

Aviation fuel is extremely volatile and burns quickly, leading to the rapid spread of fire, which will invade the fuselage almost immediately. Toxic smoke will be created and will spread quickly throughout the cabin. When the exits are opened, a so-called "chimney effect" may occur,

causing the fire to burn even more fiercely. Because the smoke and toxic gases replace the air being breathed, the passengers and crew soon become intoxicated, since oxygen will not be reaching their brains, causing disorientation, dizziness, and nausea. Their eyes may also be irritated, and breathing may be labored and painful. During the confusion and panic that follow a crash, some victims may not get to an exit, even though it may be within easy reach. Additionally, the cabin temperature may climb to thousands of degrees as the fire quickly spreads, causing more commotion as trapped individuals attempt to evacuate.

above left A control tower from where air traffic is monitored.

above Firemen examine the wreckage of a light aircraft.

below An aircraft bursts into flames as it impacts on the ground.

above Snow storms and cold weather can cause ice buildup.

right A tropical rainforest with thick canopy coverage, making it hard to carry out a search for any survivors.

Locating the craft

When the accident occurs at night, or during inclement weather, such as thick fog, fire trucks may be equipped with heat-sensitive devices allowing drivers to steer their trucks to the scene and locate the aircraft rapidly.

If an accident occurs during flight, reaching the crash scene may take time, depending on the location of the wreckage. In tropical areas, searching for an aircraft and actually reaching it may prove difficult, due to the vegetation and terrain. An example of this is the Aviateca Airlines accident of 1995, in which a flight from Miami, Florida, to San José, Costa Rica, crashed en route while about to make a stopover in San Salvador, El Salvador. The Boeing 737 crashed against the Chinchontepec Volcano, an area difficult to reach. All 68 people on board died on impact. When the bodies were eventually recovered, they were sent to the nearest morgue for autopsy and identification.

In the case of a small airplane, such as a two- or four-seater, its size and the conditions common to tropical regions mean that months, or even years, may pass before it is located and eventually recovered. Sometimes,

below The wreckage of a light plane along a riverbank.

an aircraft is discovered only because experienced hikers or hunters happen to be in the area and notify the authorities. In such instances, the human remains will normally be skeletonized when found, usually fragmented, and in most cases disarticulated within the cabin. This is due to the fragmentation of the bones caused by falling and impact injuries. As the remains decompose, the skeleton loses the connective tissue that holds the bones together, leading to disarticulation.

Some bones may exhibit superficial burning, manifested by black marks, which indicate the specific part of the body that was exposed directly to fire. Initially, the individual may have been protected by clothing, and the fire may not have been long or hot enough to calcinate the remains. The recovery of remains takes time and care, since it is important that their positions are recorded exactly. This will make the work of identification much easier when dealing with commingled remains.

The bodies of the victims of small airplane crashes are also likely to suffer animal scavenging if the search teams are unable to reach a site quickly enough. In the United States, there have been reports of small planes crashing in remote areas and the victims being scavenged by bears, to the point where the bones have been altered and the bears' teeth marks were visible. In such circumstances, the identification process is still a vital issue, and forensic anthropologists are called in to assist, since the rescue and identification is usually centered upon skeletal remains.

On the other hand, victims of air accidents are not always restricted to those inside the aircraft. In some instances, the aircraft may impact a highway, or a residential or business area, causing additional casualties on the ground. An illustration of this is the case of an Air France Concorde that was heading from Paris to New York. Upon takeoff from Charles de Gaulle International Airport in July 2000, the supersonic jet experienced difficulties when one of its engines caught fire. The incident killed all 109 passengers and crew on board, as well as five people on the ground at Gonesse, 4 miles (6 km) from the airport.

Injuries, fires, and the cause of death

The injuries suffered by an individual when involved in an air accident will depend upon the speed and the angle of the impact, as well as the type of aircraft involved. When the angle of impact is between 45 and 90 degrees, it is referred to as a head-on impact. This type of crash usually occurs at a considerable speed, and the remains of individuals may be extremely fragmented, causing severed body parts to be spread about widely at the scene. Such fragmentation may cause very small pieces of bone to become embedded in torn muscle and other types of soft tissue, making it difficult to discern different anatomical parts. In many cases, body parts may have pieces of the aircraft's wreckage embedded in them. In cases involving low-angle impacts (0–45 degrees), individuals may be fragmented, but the dispersal of body parts does not always occur.

An autopsy, performed by a forensic pathologist, will establish the cause of death. A common cause of death in an air accident is injury to the internal organs, caused by the trauma received upon impact. However, fire and smoke inhalation may also be causes of death—for example, when a plane is able to taxi on the ground, but the fire and fumes within the cabin

right French rescue personnel mark the area with cones to indicate where the position of human remains, following the Air France Concorde crash.

below Flames burst out of Concorde just before it crashed in July 2000.

reach the passengers and crew before they are able to escape. In cases of smoke inhalation, if the bodies are not severely burned, smoke in the air passages and in the lungs will be detected during the postmortem examination. In other cases, the plane may burst into flames, causing the death of those inside primarily as the result of burns.

Forensic identification team

After all the survivors have been rescued, the search for the dead begins. The scene to be covered may be extensive, since the impact of a large, heavy aircraft tends to spread wreckage and remains over a wide radius. Regardless of the size of the area, much care is usually taken to keep outsiders away from the scene by delineating the crash site with ropes. An accident scene coordinator will organize the steps to be taken, enlisting law enforcement personnel to assist with the various tasks.

The site may be investigated using a grid system, allowing it to be divided into manageable working areas, each recorded by means of photographs, written notes, video, and the use of eletronic surveying equipment. Every item recovered, whether human, personal effects, or crash debris, is always recorded for future study by the investigators. Additionally, as bodies are recovered, their specific association with other remains and artifacts assists in furthering the identification process. Usually, in the case of an airliner, an inventory of passengers and the seating arrangement exists, which greatly aids investigators as they go

below Rescue workers removing the bodies from an air crash.

about their work. Every item discovered is flagged to indicate its location, regardless of how small or fragmented it may be, since the association of artifacts with human remains may aid identification as the scene is gradually reconstructed. Usually, reconstruction of the recovered material is carried out at an airport hangar, which provides a suitably large base for the identification personnel. Refrigerated trucks may be used to store the remains of victims.

During disaster victim identification, commonly referred to as DVI, the work must be carried out with the participation of a multidisciplinary team, since in cases involving mass fatality incidents, such as air accidents, the remains may be severely fragmented and commingled. Bones may be burnt to the point of severe cracking, distorting their morphology and so slowing progress. The forensic work may be altered or reduced if the remains are difficult to recover, or if special equipment is needed to lift large sections of the aircraft, such as the fuselage, which may contain bodies.

Among the various forensic specialists present are pathologists, anthropologists, odontologists, radiologists, and fingerprint specialists. Each area of expertise would be set up within its own working station; however, fluid communication is maintained between all concerned. During DVI, the use of mobile computed tomography is advantageous, as the forensic personnel, including forensic anthropologists, can conduct the postmortem examinations more rapidly than would be the case by the use of conventional methods, such as x-rays and fluoroscopy. Additionally, it allows religious requirements to be maintained, and provides safer handling conditions for those involved.

An information center is set up to attend to the needs of the victims' families, who can also play an important role by providing information that may aid the identification process. They may be able to indicate who to contact for dental and medical records necessary to effect positive identifications. Good communication between investigators and the families of the victims will accelerate the process of identification.

Problems may be encountered when families have split up, and former spouses have remarried and have dependants under different names and at different addresses. In such cases, personnel are assigned to locate all those concerned, for both moral and legal reasons, as well as to obtain any information that may be of help in the identification process.

Once identified, the remains are returned to the victims' families. In the case of foreign nationals, after autopsy and identification, the bodies are repatriated with the aid of the appropriate consulate or embassy.

right A flight data recorder salvaged after an accident—a vital indicator in helping to determine the cause of an air accident.

Accident investigation

While the triage and recovery of the bodies is being carried out, the investigation of the cause of the accident will be underway by another group of specialists, who will need to locate the "black box." This contains recordings of everything said in the cockpit and the readouts of the various instruments up to the time of the crash. Additionally, visible structural damage to the wreckage, and the accounts of witnesses, survivors, and air traffic controllers, will all help to shed light on what may have caused the accident. Usually, the authorities involved in the investigation will be from the country in which the accident occurred. If the airline is registered overseas, the authorities from that country may become involved.

After the investigation has been completed and the remains turned over to the families, a debriefing takes place for all those involved—this is essential, since the task is intense, both physically and emotionally.

Arrow Airlines Charter

During December 1985, a Douglas DC-8 belonging to Arrow Airlines fell to the ground shortly after takingoff from Gander International Airport, Newfoundland, Canada. The disaster claimed the lives of 245 American soldiers and all eight crew members.

The soldiers were from the 101st Airborne Division and were returning to their base at Fort Campbell, Kentucky, having spent several months with the Multinational Force and Observers—a peacekeeping organization that had been working in Egypt's Sinai Peninsula.

They had departed Cairo for the United States, with two stopovers en route, the second in Canada. There, the plane was serviced and readied for the last leg of the journey. Soon after takeoff, however, it quickly began to lose altitude and descended toward Gander Lake, hitting the ground in a hilly wooded area. The plane had full fuel tanks, causing a massive fire upon impact.

All the emergency personnel deemed necessary to carry out the search and recovery at the scene were assembled rapidly. The Royal Canadian Mounted Police

left Part of the fuselage lying in a wooded area.

above Picking up the wreckage from the remains of the Arrow DC8.

opposite A hangar used as a storage facility.

participated in conjunction with military personnel from the United States, since the victims were attached to the US Army.

It was agreed that the remains would be transported to the Air Force Port Mortuary at Dover Air Force Base in the United States for autopsy. There, scientists from the Armed Forces Institute of Pathology would carry out the necessary forensic work.

The search and recovery at the disaster site proved to be a difficult task due to the intense heat created by the fire. However, the remains and personal belongings of the victims had been recovered completely within a few days. All corpses, body parts, and associated items were mapped and documented before being moved to a hangar at Gander Airport, which served as a provisional morgue. Additionally, the investigators had to document the entire crash site and the condition

of the plane, then reconstruct the events that had led to the tragedy.

Once the recovery had been completed and a final search made of the scene, the bodies were transported to Dover for forensic analysis. There, the remains were photographed, and the corresponding medical forms were properly annotated with the relevant forensic data that would assist in the identification process. All the remains were X-rayed, these radiographs being compared later with antemortem medical and dental records of the victims. Families were asked to provide any details that could help identify the victims.

Forensic anthropologists analyzed the human remains for physical characteristics, then matched these with information pertaining to each soldier. For each corpse, medical and dental records were compared with the postmortem radiographs.

Additionally, where possible, fingerprinting was used and with this approach, positive identifications were possible. Any corpses that required further examination and study were stored in refrigerated semitrailers until this could be carried out.

When the forensic analysis of all the remains had been completed, the investigators agreed that two bodies remained unaccounted for. The crash scene was searched again, and the missing remains eventually recovered. By February 1986, all the bodies had been positively identified. The result of the investigation into the cause of the accident indicated that it had occurred due to ice buildup on the airplane.

Five years after the disaster, a memorial, named the Silent Witness Monument, was erected at the crash site to commemorate those who perished there.

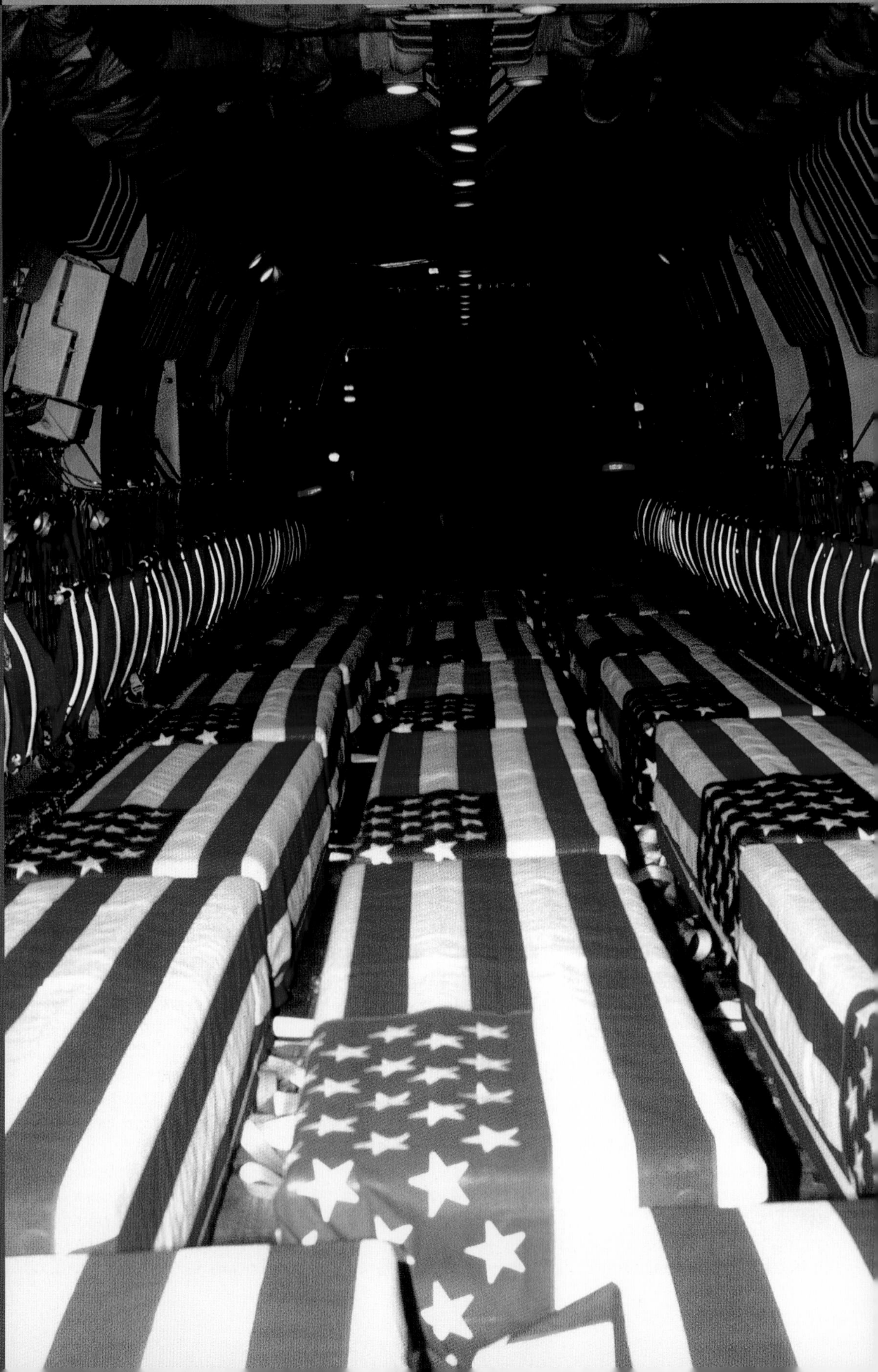

opposite The caskets containing the soldiers' remains, each draped with the United States flag.

below The Silent Witness Monument, Gander, Canada. In memory of the soldiers who died in the December 1985 aircrash.

ValuJet Flight 592

In May 1996, ValuJet Flight 592 crashed into the Florida Everglades soon after takeoff. On board the DC-9 were 110 people, including the crew, who were traveling from Miami, Florida, to Atlanta, Georgia.

The pilot reported that smoke was present in the cockpit soon after departure. It is believed that he intended to return to the airport, but the airplane nose-dived into the Everglades before he could do so.

Emergency personnel made an immediate search of the crash scene for survivors, some using airboats to aid them, but it soon became obvious that no one had survived. The impact of the jetliner caused extreme fragmentation of the fuselage and crushed the passengers within it, apparently due to the aircraft striking the limestone formations that lay under the shallow water of the swamp. Upon impact, the fuselage and human remains it contained quickly sank.

The original area of the impact was estimated at around 5,000 square feet (464.5 square meters) and as much as five feet (1.5 meters) deep. Several weeks were required to complete the search for the victims and wreckage, with the help of ground-penetrating radar.

The Everglades is a low-lying subtropical swamp with adjacent lakes and marshy areas. This made the recovery task extremely difficult due to huge amounts of decaying plant matter, and the peat that impregnates the water reduces visibility to almost zero. To make matters worse, the water was full of jet fuel hazardous to the divers. Snakes and alligators, which are native to the area, posed

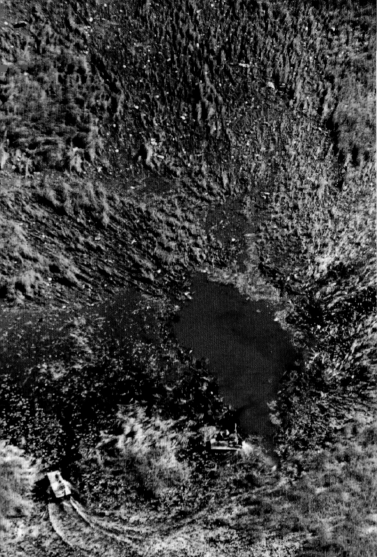

opposite top A ValuJet DC-9.

opposite bottom Investigators from the National Transportation Safety Board meet at a hangar where parts of the salvaged fuselage were stored.

left Rescue workers on airboats look for survivors in the Everglades.

below Workers wearing biohazard suits on a floating platform prepare for the dredging operation.

little threat to the search team, since they tended to stay away due to the fuel spillage. However, sporadic thunderstorms and high temperatures further hindered the search.

As a rule, those involved in the recovery worked in small groups for short shifts, often as little as 15 to 20 minutes at a time. They used hooks, rakes, and their hands to locate the remains and objects such as metal, baggage, and any personal effects that had not disintegrated. To ensure maximum efficiency in the search, a grid system was employed to divide the site into manageable areas. Heavy equipment was brought to the

scene, since some of the metal parts were too heavy to maneuver by hand.

By the end of the search, thousands of human fragments had been recovered, but no complete human body had been retrieved, with much of the wreckage unaccounted for.

The Metro-Dade Office of the Medical Examiner took charge of the autopsies. Forensic odontologists, fingerprint experts, and anthropologists all assisted, and the latter were asked to identify the children on board. As a general rule, the age of a young individual is assessed by the dental development present at the time of

death. However, cranial and dental remains had tended to sink deeper into the swamp than other body parts, and all the bodies had been extremely fragmented upon impact. Therefore, identifications were made by examining the remaining bones. One method was to take X-rays of the wristbones, since these have a distinct chronology of development throughout childhood. By assessing the development of these bones, the ages of individuals were estimated, then compared with information gathered from the victims' families and the database of those on board the doomed aircraft.

American Airlines Flight 191

On May 25, 1979, American Airlines DC-10 Flight 191 was bound from Chicago's O'Hare International Airport to Los Angeles, California. Soon after takeoff, the jetliner lost one of its engines, which hit the runway. The plane rolled on its side and, in seconds, began to nose-dive until it hit the ground and exploded. All 258 passengers, 13 crew members, and two people on the ground were killed instantly.

At the scene, rescue personnel had to wait until the fire was extinguished and the wreckage had cooled sufficiently before they could begin to recover the human remains, personal effects, and parts of the aircraft.

Due to the nature of the impact, the remains were scattered, severely fragmented, and burned. Only isolated body parts were recovered, and they could not be identified by conventional means.

This presented a serious problem, and the assistance of various forensic experts was required to identify the bodies.

As the recovery operation got underway, it became apparent that personal effects could aid in the identification of the bodies, but they were not easy to retrieve. Searchers found only fragmented small items, together with badly torn and burned clothing.

A hangar was used as a provisional mortuary. The remains were placed on tables for the forensic experts to begin their arduous task.

The identification process took several weeks and required the skills of forensic radiologists, odontologists, anthropologists, and medical examiners. Because of the poor condition of the remains, and the number of victims requiring identification, computers were used to assist the forensic work.

This air disaster was the first time a computer program was

opposite One of the jetliner's engines (on the left), lies among burned cars.

above Part of the fuselage lies next to a smashed mobile home.

employed to compare the passengers' descriptions, given by friends and families, with the forensic data available. Information on the passengers included dental characteristics, illnesses, surgical procedures, bone traumas, scars, clothing, and jewelry that may have been worn on the day of the accident. Forensic information on age, sex, and stature was entered for each set of remains. Then the program was run to match the characteristics of the victims with the sets of remains. In some cases,

bodies had similar physical characteristics and needed greater scrutiny by the scientists but, on the whole, the program helped speed up the identification process.

Once a match had been obtained, antemortem data, such as radiographs, were compared with those taken of the remains. This provided a positive identification. Although some passengers were never positively identified, the experience gained from this mass disaster has helped in the investigation of similar catastrophes.

7 Fires and Explosives

Whether or not a fire is started deliberately, an investigation needs to be set up in order to determine the motive, the extent of the damage caused, and the number of victims involved, if any. Those caught up in a fire or an explosion suffer from a variety of injuries, including smoke inhalation, blistering and, in extreme cases, death.

« Often, a fire will be started intentionally to conceal the body of an individual who has been murdered. The purpose may be to alter the remains, or to dupe the authorities into believing that the body is that of someone other than the true victim. »

For a fire to start, there must be a source of ignition in the form of a spark or other heat source, and a supply of fuel in addition to oxygen from the air (unless the fuel is selfoxidizing). Fires may be classified according to the type of combustible source involved. These include wood, paper, flammable liquids, electrical faults, and, metals such as potassium and titanium. Depending on the source, a fire will display particular characteristics, such as intensity and duration, and the method required to extinguish it will vary as a result.

When fires cause material damage, as well as loss of life, a formal investigation is usually necessary. Within the legal framework, a fire may be investigated for a variety of reasons. There is a need to establish whether it was started accidentally or was set deliberately, as in the case of arson.

Arson

Arson refers to the intentional burning of a property—for vengeance, to defraud an insurance company, to harass someone, or due to pyromania, although many other reasons exist. Individuals who suffer from pyromania start fires to satisfy an urge that they cannot control, and the affliction is classified as a mental disorder. Regardless of the reason for arson, it may result in the unintentional death of a person. In such cases, the laws of many countries dictate that, even if the arsonist is unaware that a person is inside the building when the fire was started, they will be charged with murder. In arson cases, an accelerant, such as gasoline, is frequently utilized to start the fire more rapidly. Accelerant use can be detected by employing trained dogs during the investigation.

Often, a fire will be started intentionally to conceal the body of an individual who has been murdered. The purpose may be to alter the

right The remains of Alfred Rouse's car, after it was set on fire.

remains so that the true cause of death is not discovered, or to dupe the authorities into believing that the body is that of someone other than the true victim. An example of this occurred one evening in November 1930, in Northampton, England, where a car was found on fire with a body inside. The fire was intense enough to burn the body beyond recognition. Through subsequent investigations, it was discovered that the car belonged to Alfred Rouse and, at first, it was thought that it was he who had died. A while later, however, he was spotted in Wales. Under interrogation, he admitted that the body was that of a hitchhiker whom he had picked up and then murdered. He had hoped to confuse the authorities over the identity of the body so that he could start his life again, since he was saddled with many debts, including several child support payments. Subsequently, Rouse was tried for murder and sentenced to death. However, the identity of the man in the car was never established.

The main problems with fire are that vital evidence may be rapidly destroyed and the body altered in the process of burning. Nonetheless, the different fields of forensic science have developed a variety of techniques to solve fire-related crimes. Identification of the victims may often be possible and, for this purpose, both forensic odontology and anthropology play important roles. Had forensic science been more advanced in the 1930s, it may have been possible to identify the man in the Rouse case.

Cremations

Various societies around the world have practiced cremation since ancient times, including the Greeks and Romans. In the United States, the Modocs from northern California cremated their dead on funeral pyres. When a Modoc died away from home, the body would be carried to his or her village as soon as possible, otherwise it was partially cremated so that the bones could be returned later to their final resting place.

In modern times, the practice of cremation on a pyre continues to be employed in the East, as in India. On the other hand, within Christian societies, cremation contradicted the religious belief of the bodily resurrection of the dead, and it fell out of favor. However, during the 19th

left A pyre constructed to cremate a body in India.

century, the practice was revived and today, although burial in a cemetery is still the most common way of laying the dead to rest, cremation has become more widely accepted and practiced.

In Western societies, the reason for choosing cremation may be psychological in nature or be derived from a practical decision—for example, there may be less emotion attached to the funeral process if there is no burial in the ground, or it may be simply a matter of saving land. Whatever the reasons, the demand for more crematories is rising.

Modern crematories have furnaces designed to burn bodies at temperatures ranging from 1,400°F to 2,700°F (760°C to 1,482°C) over a period of two or three hours. The body is consumed by fire and heat, becoming vaporized to the degree that only bone and tooth fragments survive the process, together with noncombustible materials such as dental metalwork, jewelry, and orthopedic pins. The remains are left for one or two hours to cool; they often weigh as little as 4 lb (1.8 kg)—the average weight for a complete body after cremation (see case study No. 26). Since the body will not have been reduced to ashes completely, it is processed mechanically to reduce the remains into smaller particles so that they may be placed in an urn. Then the ashes may be scattered later or put in a final resting place.

Small pieces of bone may still be present within the ashes, and if they are scattered in a place where they may be discovered, the police may be called to the scene in the belief that foul play has occurred. However, proper examination of the fragments by a qualified forensic anthropologist can usually clarify the situation quite easily.

Bone and tooth alterations

Thermal burn is caused by exposure to an extreme heat source, such as open flames, and can cause great damage to the human body. The degree of harm inflicted depends primarily upon the amount of exposure and the intensity of the heat source.

First-degree burning affects the outer part of the skin, but with no blistering. This is present in second-degree burns, since more damage occurs to the deeper tissue layers. Third-degree burning affects all of the available skin tissue and usually greatly impairs its regeneration. Although it is not often used, the term fourth-degree burning describes the complete incineration of the tissues over the entire surface of the body.

If an individual dies from smoke inhalation and his or her body is recovered fairly quickly after the fire has taken effect, the skin may exhibit blistering. The airways and the lungs will display evidence of smoke, and usually the individual is easy to identify by conventional means. With increased exposure and a greater intensity of heat, the skin will start to char. Furthermore, the muscles, ligaments, and tendons will all react to the fire and heat by contracting and twisting. In such cases, the hands will clench into fists, and the arms and legs will flex, much like the posture of a boxer. As the body burns further, the flexed limbs relax again. However, while the soft tissue is contracting, the bones are subjected to stress that causes them to warp and crack horizontally and lengthwise. This is unlike bones that are burned without tissue present, which exhibit only lengthwise splitting and no other alterations.

The warping of the bones must be taken into consideration when analyzing human remains. Nonetheless, with experience in bone analysis and knowledge of how fire alters the human skeleton, an accurate analysis may be completed.

Bones may shrink by up to 25 percent in size if exposed to temperatures between 1,292°F and 1,652°F (700°C and 900°C). This shrinkage must be considered when conducting a bone examination to determine factors such as the sex and age of an individual.

The color of the bones will also provide clues as to the circumstances involved. When bones are yellow or brown, it indicates that they have been exposed to low heat, and that they have retained their natural oils; other colors that may be seen on burned bones are black, gray, blue-gray, and white. Bones exhibiting a white coloration have usually been exposed to high temperatures for long periods of time, such as in a crematory, where their organic components have been dissipated totally by the cremation process.

In cases where the body remains exposed to high temperatures for long periods of time, the hands and feet may become entirely separated from the arms and legs; further prolonged exposure may cause the limbs to separate from the body as well. More severe damage occurs when the skull starts to fragment, then separates from the body. The fully cremated stage is reached when the body has no tissue left upon it at all and the bones are in small pieces. The changes that affect the bones are obvious at a glance; under the microscope, a cut section from a burned bone will clearly illustrate changes to its internal structure.

Teeth are altered by fire too, their visible condition and color indicating their fragility. When working with burned dental remains, forensic odontologists employ a series of categories: intact, when the fire has not altered the teeth; scorched, when the teeth exhibit discoloration; charred, when there is carbonization; and incinerated, which indicates that they have been reduced to ashes. If the remains of teeth are ashen gray in color, the chances are that they are exceedingly fragile, so extreme care must be taken when recovering such remains, since they may crumble when touched. When they have been altered to this extent, reconstruction is almost impossible.

At the scene and body examination

The processing of a fire scene requires the cooperation of a team of experts to deal with the diverse circumstances that may arise. Usually, firefighters, paramedics, and other rescue personnel are the first on the scene, with a triage team normally being set up as in the case of aviation accidents (see Chapter 6). The investigators will conduct a survey of the area, and the forensic fire experts will determine the cause of the fire and its starting point. If the heat was intense, forensic anthropologists will be required at the scene, since it is likely that body fragments will be recovered.

Once the remains are recovered, they are transported to a designated morgue to be examined, where the setting is the same as for air disasters (Chapter 6). The forensic pathologist will determine the cause of death; if the victims in question have not been charred or calcinated, the soft tissue from the airways of the lungs may be examined. If the lungs are free of carbon monoxide, there may be evidence of foul play and the actual cause of death must be determined by the pathologist.

A forensic odontologist or anthropologist will be required to identify severely damaged remains. The latter's examination relies on the observation of the burned remains, the color, texture, and condition, all of which can indicate whether or not the body was burned while the bone had tissue on it. Even when severely fragmented, it is possible to distinguish the section of the body to which the bones belong (see case study No. 26). The bones may also retain key identifying characteristics that will assist in determining whether the remains are those of an adult, adolescent, or child.

When the remains are analyzed by a forensic odontologist, the procedures used allow identification of the victim without markedly altering the dental remains. The odontologist will examine the teeth, then remove some of the burned soft tissue, if present, so that the characteristics of the teeth will be apparent. Teeth may be X-rayed, and impressions made of them, but as a general rule they are always photographed. Loose teeth must be identified and put into clearly labeled containers. The information obtained from the examination will then be compared with antemortem dental records to effect a positive identification.

Classification of explosives

The tactics employed by terrorist groups depend on the explosives available to them. These range from conventional types, such as TNT, to relatively recent developments, such as the plastic explosive, Semtex. The latter is stable and very safe to handle, since it needs a detonator to ignite it, but it is very difficult to trace because it does not give off an odor.

Explosives are classified in two categories: low and high. To be most effective, low explosives usually must be confined in a small space. An example of a low explosive would be gunpowder, also known as black

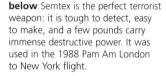

below Semtex is the perfect terrorist weapon: it is tough to detect, easy to make, and a few pounds carry immense destructive power. It was used in the 1988 Pam Am London to New York flight.

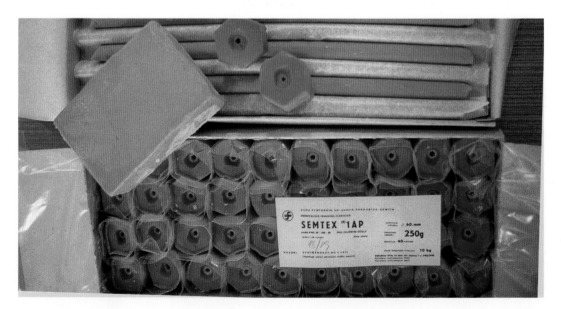

left The reconstructed cargo area of the Pan Am aircraft which exploded above Lockerbie, Scotland, in 1988.

powder. This is the oldest known explosive and is believed to have originated in China during the 10th century. The effects of low explosives can be damaging to people and structures. Much worse in their effects, however, are high explosives, such as TNT (trinitrotoluene) and dynamite, which detonate violently and easily without needing to be contained in a small space. High explosives will shatter structures, reducing them to small pieces.

Terrorism

An example of the terrorist use of plastic explosive is the Lockerbie air disaster, which occurred in December 1988. Pan Am Flight 103, en route from London to New York, exploded above the town of Lockerbie, in Scotland, at an altitude of over 30,000 feet (9,140 meters). The aircraft suffered a total breakup, which sent various sections in different directions including the cockpit, wings, engines, cabin, and tail. Damage on the ground included a large crater caused by parts of the plane as they impacted. Structures and houses were set on fire, and several people died on the ground, bringing the total number of victims to 259.

A triage was implemented at once, but no one survived the accident. The task of recovering the victims followed the normal procedure for airline accidents (see Chapter 6). The search for evidence of a bomb was difficult, since the blast had scattered the fuselage over a vast area. After much searching, and the eventual reconstruction of the aircraft and baggage compartment, it was determined that the cause of the explosion

above The smashed cockpit of Pan Am Flight 103 near Lockerbie.

opposite The World Trade Center burns behind Brooklyn Bridge, New York. In the worst attack on American soil since Pearl Harbor, two hijacked planes slammed into the Twin Towers, demolishing the two 110-story towers that symbolize US financial might.

was due to a terrorist act, and that plastic explosives had been concealed in a radio cassette player in the baggage compartment.

In the Lockerbie case, the bomb had been deposited by the perpetrators, who were not present when it went off. However, another technique utilized by terrorists is suicide bombing, when an explosive device is strapped to the body of an individual who is willing to die for the cause. The explosives are usually detonated in a public area, or on a bus, to create the maximum possible damage. In such circumstances, the body of the person carrying the explosives is often more fragmented than those of the victims, due to the proximity of the device.

On September 11, 2001, one of the most apocalyptic acts of terrorism witnessed in modern times was perpetrated upon the Twin Towers of the World Trade Center in New York City, when two commercial jetliners were commandeered by suicide hijackers and purposefully flown into the buildings.

American Airlines Flight 11, bound for Los Angeles, was hijacked by terrorists and taken off course shortly after takeoff from Boston's Logan International Airport. At approximately 0845 hours Eastern Daylight Time, the Boeing 767 was flown at full force into the north tower of the World Trade Center. Some 15 minutes later, United Airlines Flight 175 also heading to Los Angeles and hijacked by members of the same terrorist organization, was flown into the south tower.

While chaos was spreading across New York, another hijacked aircraft, United Airlines Flight 93 from Newark to San Francisco, crashed off course south of Pittsburgh, short of its intended target. Finally, a fourth hijacked airliner, American Airlines Flight 77, was plunged into the Pentagon in Washington, D.C.

Having just begun their journeys, the two ill-fated aircraft that crashed into the Twin Towers were full of aviation fuel. This meant that upon impact, a tremendous explosion was created, resulting in instant fire. The

collision caused critical structural damage to the buildings and within hours, both towers collapsed, creating an area of destruction which is now referred to as Ground Zero.

It is estimated that more than 5,000 people occupied the towers at the time, and during the morning rush hour many thousands more were on the streets in the immediate vicinity. Those on the ground fled the flying debris and many occupants on the lower levels of the building managed to escape, but others, unfortunately, did not. To add to the widespread destruction, on the evening of September 12, another building within the World Trade Center complex collapsed. Though it is believed that no further casualties arose, this subsequent blow substantially hindered the recovery process.

A triage process was immediately implemented and New York City's local authorities—including the New York Fire and Police Departments—responded rapidly in evacuating the affected areas of the city. A massive search for survivors ensued aided by 40 federal search and recovery dogs which were used to search through the mountains of rubble. As in any triage, once the survivors are rescued, the task then turns to the retrieval of those who could not be saved.

In addition to the New York Fire and Police Departments, approximately 500 trained staff assisted with the recovery work. These included burn nurses to tend to patients suffering from severe burns; pharmacists; physicians; and family assistance personnel whose role it was to conduct interviews, carry out briefings with families of the victims, and assist with taking DNA samples. Also deployed was a team of mental health counselors who provided support to the victims, their surviving relatives and friends,

below Rescue workers work at the disaster site now known as Ground Zero, where the Twin Towers once stood. It took eight months and nineteen days to clear the area.

and to the rescue workers in the aftermath of the attacks. The recovery work was conducted with the help of the US Department of Health and Human Services, liaising with Disaster Medical Assistance Teams (DMATs), Disaster Mortuary Operational Response Teams (DMORTs), and a number of other specialty teams from across the United States.

In terms of forensics, DMORTs set up a temporary morgue site complete with all the necessary equipment required for the identification process, in an empty hanger at LaGuardia airport, where they received and processed incoming remains. Their task was to provide 24-hour support to the city Medical Examiner as well as to process all post-mortem specimens received. Additionally, DMORTs were also involved in conducting family interviews, collecting records, and performing other administrative duties. Most of the wreckage from the World Trade Center site was shipped to the Staten Island Landfill where DMORT personnel stationed there sift through the debris in the hope of finding items that may lead to possible identification. DMORTs were assisted by teams of forensic anthropologists, medical examiners, fingerprint specialists, X-ray technicians, and DNA specialists.

The nature of the disaster meant that many remains were too fragmented to be identifiable by conventional methods of fingerprinting or physical recognition. The intervention of forensic anthropologists therefore played a crucial part in the retrieval of human remains at the scene, as well as in the examination of the remains at the mortuaries, working in conjunction with other experts. However, due to the extreme fragmentation of the remains, many could not easily be identified by forensic anthropologists and so the use of DNA sampling has been a priority in this case.

The authorities in the State of New York are coordinating a database of DNA samples taken from the human remains retrieved as well as samples offered by relatives who have lost their loved ones in the terrorist attack. This will allow for possible DNA matches to be made and subsequent positive identifications. To date, many victims have been positively identified; however, as time passes the number of identifications is decreasing.

It is estimated that the total number of victims who perished at the World Trade Center stands at more than 2,600; however, it is impossible to conclude a definite number of victims in a situation such as this. Furthermore, some years after the attacks, bones were still being discovered, sorted, and added to the data base, constituting the requirement for further investigations on part of the authorities.

Rescue and identification

Because bombs generally involve a high number of fatalities, a team is usually assembled to search for both survivors and bodies. The area is sealed off to preserve any evidence that could help the experts determine the type of bomb employed. Additionally, a police or military bomb squad decides if the area is safe for those involved in the rescue and recovery process.

Israel has considerable experience of dealing with such acts, and the authorities there have developed a procedure to cope with them. After a bombing, the emergency rooms of nearby hospitals are put on alert, and religious leaders and psychologists are brought in to help survivors and victims' families deal with the trauma.

above The aftermath of a terrorist attack in Jerusalem in March 1996. Twenty people died in the bomb attack.

The positions of bodies and body parts are recorded, as are those of any personal effects so that they may be correlated to specific individuals during the identification process. Unlike other countries, where pathologists and anthropologists are present at the scene, in Israel these professionals remain where the autopsies and identification take place. The reason for this is that those involved at the scene in the manipulation of the remains are Orthodox Jewish volunteers. Their activities are considered to be a sacred duty under the Jewish tradition, because all tissue and blood must be present when the victims are laid to rest.

An information center is set up to gather data to assist families wanting information. Additionally, it collects information from families to assist in identifying the victims, such as details of scars, physical characteristics, and other dental or medical data. It is also necessary for the center to maintain a line of communication between the morgue and the hospitals. This is important, since the hospitals may be treating survivors who have lost limbs in the explosion, which must be taken into consideration when attempting to allocate body parts in the morgue.

Many different specialists examine the human remains. By X-raying the bodies, or utilizing CT scanning, any shrapnel lodged within them is found and may be passed to the investigators. This helps to determine the type of device used, as well as to reconstruct the event. Identification of the victims the skills of forensic odontologists and anthropologists, among others. DNA testing helps in the accurate association of body parts. Blood may be taken from relatives and compared with DNA extracted from the remains. When compatibility is confirmed, a positive identification may be achieved. Such is the expertise of the Israelis in this field that the process of identification can be completed in approximately 24 hours.

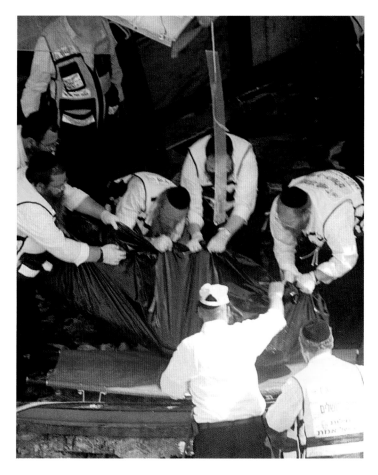

left Israeli personnel attending the scene after a suicide bombing in August 2001 in Jerusalem, killing an estimated 15 people.

below A suicide bomber decides to detonate a bomb in a busy area of Tel Aviv, Israel, in 1996, killing himself and 12 others.

Timothy McVeigh

In 1995, on a sunny spring morning in Oklahoma City, Oklahoma, Timothy McVeigh parked a Ryder rental truck containing homemade explosives produced from ammonium nitrate, a type of fertilizer, in front of the Alfred P. Murrah federal building.

When the explosives were detonated, the building was turned into a ball of fire. All its nine floors were devastated, sending glass and concrete flying. The front of the building was destroyed completely, while the blast created a crater eight feet (2.4 meters) deep and 20 feet (six meters) in diameter. Eventually, some of the floors began to collapse on top of each other. This was the first terrorist bombing ever recorded in the United States.

Aside from housing federal offices, the Murrah building also contained a day care center called "America's Kids" on its second floor, which had an enrolment of over 30 children. At the time of the blast, the center was full of workers, visitors, and children. As the rescue teams arrived at the scene, they were confronted with a truly horrific situation—survivors were trapped in the rubble, and the bodies of the dead were spread across the site. Some victims had been mutilated by the impact of the explosion, many having their clothing ripped off. Undetonated fertilizer covered the bodies and wreckage.

The rescue required the use of trained dogs from teams throughout the United States. With the aid of German shepherd dogs, golden retrievers, and bloodhounds, the survivors and the dead were located. Additionally, sounding devices were utilized to locate survivors buried underneath the rubble.

A triage system was set up so that survivors could be assessed and sent to the appropriate hospitals for treatment as soon as possible. However, the rescuers' task was not free of risk, since the building had been severely damaged and was in danger of collapsing. Yet over 500 people were rescued.

Because of the nature of the devastation, the search proved to be a long process, taxing both the rescue personnel and the dogs. They worked in shifts of approximately 12 hours at a time, and the emotional toll on those involved was high. It was difficult

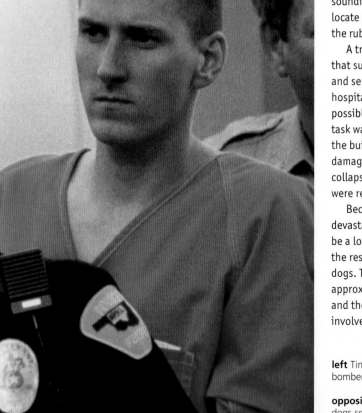

left Timothy McVeigh, the Oklahoma bomber.

opposite Rescue workers and trained dogs search the rubble of the Alfred P. Murrah federal building for possible survivors.

to grasp the immensity of the destruction and the loss of life.

The forensic teams identified the dead bodies by means of dental and bone remains. A family center was set up to provide information to the victims' relatives. In turn, the families helped by supplying details that assisted in the identification of the victims, such

as descriptions of scars and tattoos, as well as the sources of dental and medical records.

In 2001, Timothy McVeigh was executed by lethal injection at the United States Penitentiary, Terre Haute, Indiana, a facility constructed for male federal offenders on death row. The relatives of the victims were given

the opportunity of watching his execution by means of a closed-circuit TV system. Some opted to attend, but others declined, feeling that it would not help to ease the pain of losing their loved ones. A memorial has since been created at the site, with 168 chairs in remembrance of the men, women, and children who died.

above Aerial view of the extent of the damage caused to the federal building.

right Memorial to the 168 who died in the 1995 bombing.

The Hinton Rail Collision

In February 1986, in the foothills of the Rocky Mountains of Alberta, one of the worst rail disasters in Canadian history took place. Early in the morning, an eastbound Via Rail Super Continental passenger train, en route to Edmonton, collided head-on and at high speed with a westbound Canadian National freight train.

The freight train consisted of three diesel locomotives pulling over 110 cars, loaded with grain, sulfur, sodium hydroxide, ethylene dichloride, and metal pipes, among other types of freight. Although also pulled by three diesel locomotives, the passenger train was far smaller and lighter, being made up of 11 cars. On board were business people and tourists, who had no idea of the events that were about to befall them.

The collision caused the locomotives of the freight train to ride up over the top of the passenger train, leading to many of the cars being pushed together. Some of them were telescoped, whereas others were totally crushed. As the passenger cars were torn apart, glass shattered, and seats and other furnishings were thrown about.

Aside from the physical damage caused to the cars, spilt diesel fuel and other flammable substances quickly ignited into a blazing inferno, a fire that smoldered for several days. The situation rapidly became even more deadly when the ethylene dichloride began to burn, emitting deadly vapors.

The scene was chaotic, but miraculously there were survivors, who managed to pull themselves from the wreckage and eventually went to the assistance of those who were severely injured. Among the injuries sustained were serious lacerations, mutilations, and burns. Some survived only because grain spilling from the freight train put the fire out as it fell on them.

Emergency crews arrived at the scene shortly after the accident and assisted with the evacuation of the injured, who were quickly transported by land and air to appropriate hospitals. The task of recovering and identifying the dead had yet to be accomplished.

A center was soon set up to receive the families and friends of missing passengers. They were asked to provide physical details of the missing individuals. The data required included particular characteristics, such as scars, congenital defects, birthmarks, tattoos, and possible clues as to the clothing that may have been

right Fire fighters spray water over the smoldering mass of debris.

opposite Passenger cars lie commingled with freight cars in the foothills of the Rocky Mountains.

worn on the day of the accident. Inquiries were made about items of personal jewelry that the travelers were known to have worn, and medical and dental records were sought to aid the identification process. One of the major drawbacks hindering the identification of some of the victims was that there was no accurate record of the number of passengers on board the train. Unlike airlines, which keep lists of those on board, train companies do not. Therefore, ascertaining exactly how many people had been on the train at the time of the accident became very difficult.

Many of the passengers could not be identified by conventional means, since their bodies had been severely mutilated. Some retained very little flesh due to burning,

occasionally to the point of calcination; meanwhile others suffered damage from the caustic substances carried by the freight train. Forensic anthropologists from the University of Alberta were called in and given the task of identifying these remains. They worked in conjunction with the medical examiner and forensic odontologists.

The search for remains was carried out by applying forensic archeological techniques, the site being mapped and recorded sequentially as the remains and any personal belongings were recovered. The work was not easy, since the fragmented remains were mixed with the debris from the crash, and many fires were still burning, despite freezing weather.

Nonetheless, the recovery procedures were carried out and completed in nine days. In the process, anthropologists sifted through tons of debris and analyzed tens of thousands of bone fragments, which varied in size and were often commingled.

Since the recovery was carefully mapped as it progressed, personal belongings associated with particular human remains were of great assistance in identifying individuals. Further clues were provided by comparing the forensic data (such as sex, age, and stature) with the information provided by families and friends.

The multidisciplinary approach resulted in the identification of all the passengers killed, regardless of the fragmentation and distortion of the remains that were analyzed.

David Koresh

David Koresh headed the Branch Davidians, a religious sect originally formed by dissatisfied members of the Seventh-Day Adventists Church, but which had grown through the recruitment of others who wished to follow Koresh's teachings. Koresh was extremely knowledgeable about the Bible, and at times made prophesies of things to come. He often referred to himself as Jesus Christ and the Messiah.

The sect occupied a ranch situated east of Waco, Texas. Owned outright by the Davidians, the property spread over 70 acres (28 hectares) of land, on which was a massive building where they carried out their everyday activities. Within the building was a bunker containing survival items, such as food, and a considerable amount of weaponry and ammunition.

Early in 1993, agents from the ATF (Department of Alcohol, Tobacco, Firearms and Explosives) approached Koresh and his followers outside the compound, wishing to serve them with a search warrant for illegal possession of firearms and explosives. The Branch Davidians opened fire, killing four ATF agents and wounding others. The agents returned fire, and within the compound, Koresh was wounded and many others were killed. Those who perished within the compound were buried in one of the rooms, and an additional grave was created outside.

Negotiations continued over many days, some of Koresh's followers electing to leave the compound. But he remained resolute and would not give in to pressure to leave. The federal authorities continued to lay siege to the ranch, and some of the sect's members who surrendered indicated that the sanitary conditions inside the compound were becoming increasingly poor.

On April 19, the FBI called on the Branch Davidians to surrender because they were about to fire tear gas into the building, but the Davidians ignored the warning. Tear gas was thrown into the compound and, in due course, gunfire erupted. The FBI's armored vehicles then started to punch holes through the walls and a fire broke out, which spread rapidly. A few of the Davidians escaped to safety, but the majority were trapped inside and perished in the flames.

In the aftermath, it became apparent to the authorities that a multidisciplinary approach was needed to recover and identify the human remains within the compound. The work involved the participation of a variety of forensic experts, including anthropologists, odontologists, medical examiners, and criminologists.

The recovery of the human remains proved to be somewhat difficult, due to the poor condition of the building after the fire and because large quantities of live ammunition were lying around. There was also great uncertainty as to the number of victims within the compound and bunker. Consequently, the recovery operation was not conducted for several days, causing some of the bodies that had not become calcinated to decompose.

Forensic archeological techniques were applied, the investigators working meticulously through the debris. As the remains and any artifacts associated with them were found, they were photographed and recorded in context with the rest of the scene. Then the bodies were placed in body bags and transported to the Tarrant County Medical Examiner's Office in Fort Worth, Texas, where analysis of the corpses was carried out.

The remains were in a state of fragmentation, and were also calcinated, decomposed, and

left David Koresh, head of the Branch Davidians.

opposite top The Branch Davidian compound on fire, April 1993.

opposite bottom left Investigators at the site searching for bodies and remains.

opposite bottom right Bodies of the victims being removed from the compound.

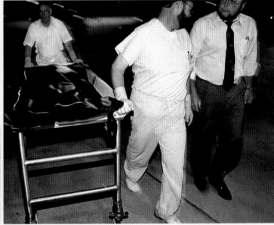

commingled. The first task of the forensic anthropologists was to sort the bones to determine how many victims there were. Some of the remains had to be reconstructed due to the amount of bone fragmentation. Once reconstructed, the anthropologists examined the morphology and development degree of the remains, as well as measuring them to determine age, sex, height, ancestry, and other characteristics for each victim. Once the characteristics were obtained, they were matched with a list of those believed to have perished in the compound.

Using dental records, forensic odontologists were able to compare antemortem records with the dental remains recovered at the site and match for positive identification. Additionally, forensic pathologists used medical records to carry out comparisons with the remains recovered.

The analysis of the human remains resulted in positive identifications of the individuals who had died, including David Koresh—who had been shot in the head—his wife, and children. The toxicological analysis performed on Koresh's tissue samples indicated

that he had inhaled toxic fumes and was, therefore, alive when the fire started. Among Koresh's followers were victims of all ages and ancestry. The traumas observed upon the bodies had been caused by shrapnel, gunshot, and fire, the heat of which had caused many of the bones to crack. Under their respective areas of expertise, the professionals involved in the investigation were able to identify 86 victims in total. Fingerprinting was one of the various processes utilized, and identifications were also made by molecular biologists who applied DNA analysis.

Cremated Bodies

When archeologists excavate ancient sites, anthropologists are given the task of examining any skeletal remains that are recovered; in many instances, these will have been cremated as a way of disposing of the dead. This practice was followed by many cultures throughout ancient Britain, where human remains have been found that exhibit varying degrees of burning.

In the region of East Anglia, an archeological site was recently excavated that was dated to between the first and third centuries AD, placing it within the period of the Roman occupation. The Roman Empire spread throughout many parts of Europe, and Britain was invaded in 55 BC, when the empire was under the rule of Julius Caesar. Through the centuries, the process of Romanization gradually took place, and Roman enclaves, including quite large urban areas, were established throughout the country, in what are today London, York, and Bath. The Celtic tribes of Britain had adopted many aspects of Roman life, including regular bathing, the drinking of imported wine, and trading throughout the Roman Empire. Nonetheless, they continued to cremate their dead, as they had done in the past.

The site excavated in East Anglia had been a small town that had become Romanized, in the territory of a tribe known as the Trinovantes. It was surrounded by fields in which cremations had been deposited in several clusters.

The cremated remains, which exhibited varying degrees of burning, were examined by anthropologist Dr. Corinne Duhig. She passed them first through a sieve with a mesh of $^3/_{16}$ in (4 mm), then one with a $^3/_{32}$-in (2-mm) mesh. The small pieces that fell through the finer mesh were set aside, since they were too small to analyze easily. The fragments retrieved from each sieve were sorted by body region. The different groups of bones were weighed to determine how complete they were. The total

average weight of a complete skeleton when fully cremated is between 3½ lb and 4½ lb (1.5 kg and 2.0 kg), and of this, the skull represents 18.2 percent, the torso 23.1 percent and the extremities 58.7 percent.

The fragments were examined more closely and, where possible, sex and age were determined, as well as any pathologies.

In one case, the remains discovered in an urn were white in color and the fragments were large, which indicated to the anthropologist that the funeral pyre had been well tended, the fire being hot enough to reduce the bones to inorganic matter only.

Additionally, it indicated that the remains had not been stirred or handled while hot, since this would have broken them into much smaller fragments. The weight of these remains was a little under 3½ lb (1.5 kg), which indicated that the body was complete.

By contrast, the remains of another individual were barely burned, the color of the bones being brown, and only a few fragments from the skull and chest area were present when sieved. The weight of these remains was only a little over 1½ lb (0.7 kg), and the remains had been disposed of simply by

depositing them on the ground, where they had become mixed with the soil. The findings indicated that, in this case, the fire had not been well tended and the remains had been carelessly gathered after the cremation.

Such procedures have been used for many years to analyze cremated remains from archeological sites. Yet the same techniques are put to use in the forensic field—for example, in cases involving homicide, in which the intentional burning and grinding or crushing of a body have taken place, to conceal the cause of death as well as the true identity of the victim.

opposite Small cremated skull fragments.

above Trays and sieves containing various bone fragments, sorted according to size.

right Small bone fragments, sieved through a 2-mm mesh.

8 Human Rights

History is littered with ruthless acts of violence against the human race. The perpetrators of these heinous crimes take no prisoners with countless innocent people, including children and pregnant women, among their victims. In some cases, it is only several years later that the true extent of the atrocities committed is discovered. It is in such cases that the expertise of forensic anthropologists becomes invaluable in the retrieval and identification of victims, so that their remains can be laid to rest in a proper manner.

The Universal Declaration of Human Rights was envisaged by the United Nations in 1948. This declaration enshrined a series of rights to which it is deemed all people are entitled. These include the rights to life, liberty, education, and equality before the law, as well as freedom of movement, unhindered affiliation to religious groups, access to information, and a personal nationality. But in the years since this declaration, a multitude of abuses against human rights have occurred, often causing the deaths of millions of innocent people.

Although human rights abuses have occurred throughout recorded history, today the public has become progressively aware of, and sensitive to, human rights issues around the world. People are persecuted for a variety of reasons, including religious belief, ethnicity, national or political affiliation, and ideology. Victims include both adults and children.

Regardless of the reasons for persecution, when it is enacted in a premeditated and systematic manner to kill, cause bodily or mental harm, to reduce living conditions to a detrimental level, to prevent individuals from having children, or to abduct children, it is described as genocide. The term "genocide" is derived from the Greek word genos, meaning "race," and cide, from the Latin, meaning "killing," hence literally "the killing of races." Methods employed to annihilate a particular group include the denial of the basic elements of existence (such as food and water), forced detention or labor, torture, starvation, and execution.

In cases of political persecution, people may be held illegally in clandestine detention centers or camps, where they may be tortured, even in the presence of family members. Victims may be held for months, or even years, enduring the full horror of their condition before possibly being released. In most cases, however, they are killed and subsequently buried in individual or mass graves, with no personal identification upon their persons, thus hampering any investigation into the causes of their deaths. One organization that works for the prevention of political persecution, torture, and execution is Amnesty International, formed in 1961 in the UK. In 1977, it won the Nobel Peace Prize.

When political persecution takes place, Amnesty International defines individuals who are taken against their will as "disappeared," meaning that they are detained by government agencies. For example, in Argentina between 1976 and 1983, thousands of people went missing because of their political beliefs during the term of the military dictatorship (see case study No. 29). Alternatively, the term "missing" is applied when people are taken by nongovernmental organizations.

« Forensic anthropology has made an immense contribution to the investigations of crimes against humanity, by identifying the bodies of victims retrieved from unmarked individual graves, as well as from mass graves, the latter often containing hundreds of bodies. »

left Adolf Hitler: a 20th century architect of genocide policies.

The 20th century

During the 20th century, the world witnessed a range of large-scale atrocities perpetrated against different groups of people. One horrific example occurred in China and is popularly referred to as "The Rape of Nanking." As the Japanese sought to extend their empire in Asia during the 1930s, their army battled with different nations, including China. In 1937, the Japanese invaded the city of Nanking, where they carried out a mass genocide upon the civilian population and the Chinese Army.

The soldiers became POWs (prisoners of war) and were killed first, followed by the systematic annihilation of civilians. Some were tied up, soaked with gasoline, and burned alive. Others were killed by machinegun fire, bayoneting, drowning, strangulation, or decapitation. Before being killed, women and young girls were often sexually abused and raped, even when pregnant. Properties were looted before being destroyed. During this orgy of death and destruction, approximately 300,000 people perished.

While such atrocities were being committed in China, the Hitler regime in Germany, which lasted from 1933 to 1945, targeted selected groups of people for persecution, imprisonment, and death. One of Hitler's

objectives was to create a "master race", in which only individuals with supposedly pure Aryan traits of blond hair, blue eyes, white skin, and the proper lineage were considered intelligent and worthy of reproducing. The antithesis of this concept, according to the Nazi regime, were the Jews.

The Jewish community had enjoyed the same rights as other German citizens until the Nuremberg Laws were enacted in 1935. These stripped German Jews of their rights and led to their ostracization within Germany, to the point where every Jew was required by law to wear a yellow Star of David. Hitler blamed the Jews for anything and everything negative that happened to the Nazi state.

In north-west Spain during 1937, the Basque town of Guernica was attacked by military aircraft of the German air force, or Luftwaffe, which was operating covertly in Spain under the moniker of the Condor Legion; Italian planes functioning as the Aviazione Legionaria were also involved. This military venture, Operation Rügen as it was known, was co-ordinated in league with Nationalist forces under the command of General Franco during the Spanish Civil War (1936-1939) (see Case study No. 31). Assistance had been requested by the Nationalists from the German and

left Bombed out buildings in Guernica, destroyed by a blitz during the Spanish Civil War.

Italian fascist governments to break the civilian and Republican military will to resist further conflict, and to bring fighting on the ground to a quicker conclusion. A variety of munitions were deployed during the air raids, including explosive and incendiary types, which were used in large quantities with the objective of causing death, chaos and destruction of a town's infrastructure. The number of victims who perished during the air raid and in its aftermath has long been disputed, ranging from a couple of hundred to thousands.

The event was memorialized by the Spanish artist Pablo Picasso in a famous painting of the same name. Operations by the Condor Legion and Aviazione Legionaria during the Spanish Civil War were widespread, including several operations against Madrid. By operating covertly as the Condor Legion, the Nazi government used the Spanish war as a proving ground for its latest military technologies. This permitted the refinement of the Luftwaffe's doctrines of aerial attack, with particular reference to strategic bombing. The manner of such aerial attacks was new in the field of warfare. Areas harbouring large and concentrated civilian populations were purposefully chosen, creating the maximum degree of rapid destruction, with the ensuing fear and panic designed to quickly break morale. Nazi Germany put the experience gained in Spain to highly effective use in several successive military operations in Continental Europe. These Blitzkrieg, or "lightning war," campaigns eventually ignited World War II in 1939.

Members of foreign forces who died during operations in Spain were given military burials there. However, the award of campaign medals and honors was delayed until it was politically expedient to distribute them, so as not to provoke untimely responses from other European countries against the actions of the fascist German and Italian governments.

After the outbreak of World War II, which followed the German invasion of Poland, the Germans began to invade other European nations, where native Jews and other ethnic groups were persecuted, arrested, and confined in concentration camps. Hitler's government imprisoned millions of people in Germany, Austria, Poland, and the Soviet Union, which then included the Ukraine. After the invasion of Poland, Jews were quickly identified and no food provisions made for them. Some were made to clean the streets and sidewalks under the supervision of German SS soldiers.

Although the total number is not known, it is estimated that tens of millions of Jews were arrested and sent to concentration camps, such as Auschwitz, Treblinka, Sobibor, and Belzec in Poland, and Buchenwald in Germany. In these camps, entire families were split up and stripped of their dignity, then starved and worked to death. Some were subjected to medical experiments by individuals, such as Dr Joseph Mengele, who became popularly known as the "Angel of Death." Others were killed in large gas chambers, in which up to 2,500 people were crammed at a time. Guards threw in pellets of Zyklon B gas, containing cyanide, through vents in the roofs. Cyanide gas was released as soon as the pellets were exposed

below A concentration camp in Auschwitz.

left Adolf Eichmann was executed for his crimes by the state of Israel in 1962.

to the air, poisoning everyone inside the chamber. The bodies of the victims were usually discovered in a "pyramid," since they had endeavored to climb to the top of the chamber in a vain attempt to escape. Other prisoners were either hanged or shot dead. Jews were selected for the task of removing and disposing of the bodies, but some refused, preferring to die instead of performing such tasks. The disposal of the remains was accomplished by cremation, or by creating huge mass graves. Few inmates of the camps survived, but those who did were often emaciated, weighing as little as 92 lb (42 kg), and desperately ill.

This particular genocide is now referred to as the Holocaust. After the war, the Nuremberg Trials of 1946 led to certain Nazis being indicted for war crimes. Some were executed, whereas others were sentenced to life imprisonment. Adolf Eichmann, an Austrian Nazi and official of the SS (the military wing of the Nazi Party), played an active role in the Holocaust, overseeing the camps and organizing mass exterminations. After the war, he escaped to Argentina, but was subsequently abducted by Israeli agents. Once in Israel, he was tried for war crimes and was hanged in 1962. Another Nazi, who escaped from Germany, was Joseph Mengele. He also fled to South America, but never stood trial for the atrocities he committed (see Chapter 5). Hitler too escaped justice by committing suicide, shooting himself just before the end of the war.

Since World War II, there have been other notable crimes against humanity. Between 1975 and 1979, some 2,000,000 people lost their lives in Cambodia under the control of Pol Pot's Khmer Rouge. Pol Pot was born in 1925, at Saloth Sar, in a rural area of Cambodia, when the country was under French colonial rule. He won a scholarship to study in France and left Cambodia during the late 1940s. In France, he became obsessed with communist ideology. Shortly after his return to Cambodia, the country became an independent nation, and Pol Pot soon became involved with the Communist Party. Eventually, he retreated to the jungle to develop his plans to take over the country, although many years would pass before he would put them into practice.

During 1975, after the Vietnam War had drawn to a close, Pol Pot and the Khmer Rouge seized the capital of Cambodia, and Pol Pot became prime minister. The country was sealed off from the outside world, and the population put to work on the land. Even those who had no experience of agricultural work were forced to fulfil Pot's ideals of agrarian communism and the rejection of the modern lifestyle. In the work camps, Cambodians were forced to labor long hours, with limited food, causing many to die of starvation and exhaustion. Those who attempted to eat while harvesting crops were killed, whereas others were tortured, and then executed.

right Pol Pot, the leader of the Khmer Rouge, responsible for the deaths of millions of Cambodians.

below Bodies found in a prison north-west of Phnom Penh, Cambodia.

left A testament of the "Killing Fields" in Cambodia.

below Photographs of Khmer Rouge victims at the Toul Sleng Genocide Museum in Cambodia.

right Remains at the site of a mass grave in Hilla, 60 miles (95 km) south of Baghdad, Iraq.

below A journalist takes video of human bones discovered from a mass grave in the suburb of Kabul, Afghanistan, in 2006.

This genocide took place in what are referred to today as the "Killing Fields," ending only with the Vietnamese invasion of Cambodia in 1979, causing Pol Pot to flee. He was never tried for his crimes against humanity, and he died in 1998 of heart failure, in a remote area of Cambodia. During 1980, mass graves were uncovered that revealed the full horror of the Khmer Rouge regime.

In the meantime, South American countries such as Chile, Uruguay, and Argentina also suffered military oppressions in the 1970s (see case studies Nos. 28 and 29). The civilian populations of those countries lived under constant violence and repression. Elsewhere, in Ethiopia, during the regime of Colonel M. H. Marian, which lasted from the 1970s to the early 1990s, the population suffered massive violations of human rights. During the 1990s, the former Yugoslavia was torn apart by a series of conflicts that resulted in the deaths of thousands of civilians and laid waste to Bosnia-Herzegovina, Croatia, and Kosovo. Other abuses occurred during the mid- and late-1990s, when mass killings were carried out in the Democratic Republic of Congo by the Kabila regime, which was subsequently investigated by the United Nations. The genocide in Rwanda claimed the lives of nearly 800,000 people in only 100 days (see case study No. 27). All these crimes have been investigated by human rights groups, aided by the skills of forensic anthropologists.

In more recent times, the wars in Iraq and Afghanistan have sparked a huge rise in atrocious human rights violations, characterized by the deaths of many innocent civilians, many of whom have been buried in mass graves. Attempts have been made to access areas within Iraq where such

above Iraqi officials remove bodies of Iraqi fighters from a mass grave in Baghdad, Iraq. The bodies were removed in 2003 so that they could be buried in a cemetery.

burials have occurred. But the frequency of undiscovered concealed ordinances has drastically restricted the scope for attempting such missions. In the case of Afghanistan, local personnel are being trained by the NGO Physicians for Human Rights to conduct the required forensic tasks including the retrieval and processing of the deceased in an appropriate manner.

Forensic involvement

Dr. Clyde Snow, a respected forensic anthropologist, initiated the systematic forensic investigation of human rights violations. He trained other individuals in his specialty in Argentina during the presidency of Raul Alfonsin, the founder of the National Commission on the Disappeared. The aim of this organization was to investigate abductions by agencies of

the previous military government. The commission requested the intervention of the American Association for the Advancement of Science and, in response, Dr. Snow and other forensic scientists stepped in. Snow taught anthropology and archeology to medical students, instructing them how to exhume bodies in the correct manner, using forensic archeological techniques, and showing them the standard methods for identifying the deceased. In 1984, Snow's students formed the Argentine Forensic Anthropology Team, the first of its kind in the world (see case study No. 29).

Since its creation, forensic scientists, including anthropologists, from around the world have become involved in the investigation of human rights violations, searching for the dead, many of whom disappeared a long time ago. As a result, victims have been recovered, identified, and

left International forensic experts examine a mass grave in Bosnia.

given the dignity of proper burial. Their families have also gained comfort from knowing the whereabouts of their loved ones. Furthermore, the scientists' work made it possible to compile evidence of atrocities. This evidence was then submitted to international criminal courts, including the International Criminal Tribunal for the Former Yugoslavia at The Hague, in the Netherlands, and the International Criminal Tribunal for Rwanda in Arusha, Tanzania, where some of those responsible have faced justice. At the time of writing, other cases remain pending, awaiting trial.

Retrieving the bodies

Forensic anthropology has made an immense contribution to the investigations of crimes against humanity by identifying the bodies of victims retrieved from unmarked individual graves, as well as from mass graves—the latter often containing hundreds of bodies.

The creation of mass graves has not been restricted to modern times, however. Such burials have also been discovered in Europe, and usually came about because of epidemics, such as the Great Plague, causing thousands of deaths. In Provence, France, it was introduced in 1720 by a ship that had arrived from Syria. The resulting epidemic killed nearly 100,000 people, and many mass graves were dug to bury the dead as quickly as possible. In Marseilles, the Plague claimed approximately 50,000 lives. One grave, dating from 1722, was excavated in 1994 by French and American scientists using specialized archeological techniques. One interesting discovery was that some of the bodies had bronze pins in their toes, which had been used to verify their death and to avoid live burials.

The same archeological techniques are applied to the excavation and exhumation of bodies in mass graves that have been created in more recent times. This is because hundreds of bodies may be present, often commingled and skeletonized, making retrieval difficult. In such instances, it may take considerable time to remove each body, even when several forensic anthropologists and archeologists are working together.

right Former Rwanda army Colonel Theoneste Bagosora [right] arrives at the International Criminal Tribunal for Rwanda in December 2007. He was convicted of charges of genocide and sentenced to life in prison. Some 800,000 Tustsi and moderate Hutus were killed as a result of the genocide.

in Basile 1633
died. 20000

in Trent. 1634
died 30000

A relatively recent mass grave may contain bodies in varying stages of decomposition. Here, the anthropologists are likely to employ different techniques to analyze and remove each body. When the remains are skeletonized, careful consideration must be given to sorting the bones without moving them from their original positions. Before removal, regardless of a body's condition, a brief assessment may be made of the age, sex, and any other details that are apparent at the time. If clothing is present, it will also be noted. All of this information can be recorded under a cataloging number by the archeologist overseeing the work. With the use of a Total Station, an archeological digital surveying tool that aids in recording accurately location, distance, and depth, the information can be put on to a computer; some of the computers are small enough to be handheld. This digital equipment allows the process to be accelerated, but with accurate results. The data is recorded, together with each body's orientation and depth within the grave, to establish a detailed three-dimensional map of the bodies and any related artifacts.

However, not all victims of human rights violations are buried. Sometimes, they are discovered lying in their homes, on the surface of

above An engraving illustrating the effects of the Plague in Europe at the beginning of the 17th century.

the ground, in rivers or within caves, among other places. Therefore, access to remains may be extremely problematical; in some cases, only one or two individuals may gain access.

The method of retrieval employed will depend on individual circumstances (see case study No. 27). Usually, bodies have been exposed to the elements for a lengthy time, and are discovered incomplete, skeletonized, commingled, and dispersed over a given area, often exhibiting the effects of animal scavenging. It may be extremely difficult to accurately determine the number of victims. Attempts may be made by establishing the minimum number of individuals (MNI), which is determined by counting the bones most represented at the scene, for example, the skulls or the femora. Although this method is not totally accurate, it remains an option to forensic anthropologists.

Once the bodies have been removed from a grave, they are taken to a morgue, which, in many cases, will be a provisional facility. There, each will be X-rayed, then a forensic pathologist will conduct the autopsy to determine the cause of death. During the autopsy, if the bodies are severely fragmented, due to the weaponry used against the victim, forensic anthropologists will work in conjunction with the pathologist, piecing together the body parts. In this manner, the pathologists will be

below A Bosnian Muslim woman mourns at her husband's grave at the Potocari Memorial Cemetery near Srebrenica, in August 2011. More than 4,500 bodies were buried there after being excavated from mass graves in Eastern Bosnia and positively identified.

able to more accurately determine the type of trauma, point of impact, and nature of the damage which has been caused, thus allowing confirmation of the cause and manner of death. Subsequently, the biological identification of each victim may be attempted by the forensic anthropologist, followed by the use of techniques such as DNA analysis to effect a positive identification.

The cause of death may vary from one situation to another. Weapons utilized to kill civilians vary with respect to the degree of direct access to them. Another important factor is the willingness of potential perpetrators to be motivated by political gain. For instance, during the Balkan War (1991–2002) the actors were heavily armed with modern weaponry, whereas in Rwanda and El Salvador machetes were used against civilians, alongside modern military hardware.

The work of both the forensic pathologist and anthropologist is a crucial element of transitional justice which any civilian population is entitled to after events of such a nature. It is through this process that the survivors and descendents of victims can understand past events, gain monetary compensation, and come to a conclusion as to a person's fate, whereupon the remains may be returned to the family for a final and proper burial.

below A Total Station on a tripod.

Genocide

Essentially, the population of Rwanda, a small country in Central Africa, is composed of three ethnic groups: the Hutus, the Tutsis, and the Twa. During Belgian colonial rule, the Tutsis enjoyed a life of privilege, and obtained good jobs and education.

This situation changed during the early 1960s, when the country gained its independence, and the Hutus gained a better position. In 1973, they came to political power for the first time. In 1994, when the Hutu president was killed in an aviation disaster, Hutu extremists accused the Tutsis of being responsible, and the "cleansing" of Inyenzi "cockroaches," as the Hutus called the Tutsis, began in earnest. The genocide was carried out for the most part using pangas, machete-like tools widely employed in agriculture. Pangas were used to mutilate, kill, or injure people and stop them from escaping—a victim who attempted to get away would be struck in the ankle area with a panga, severing the Achilles tendon. This would make it impossible for the person to run or walk. Some individuals exhibited defense wounds in the form of cuts to the fingers, which had been received as the victim attempted to shield his or her face. No one was spared, and throughout the country entire families were killed. The fields and streets of Kigali, the capital, were littered with bodies and stained with pools of blood.

Some individuals hid in small spaces in houses, such as between the roof and the ceiling. They would stay there for days on end, with no food or water. Many managed to survive, but others were discovered and were killed. Even when they sought refuge in Catholic churches, they were often trapped inside and murdered.

This was the most intense genocide of the 20th century, since it is estimated that around 800,000 people died in a matter of 100 days. The victims were quickly buried in mass graves to prevent diseases from spreading and because this was the most sensible way of disposing of so many bodies. Moreover, since entire families had perished, there was often no one to claim the bodies.

One of the many communities devastated by the genocide was Kibuye, a small settlement on Lake Kivu, in the western part of the country. In 1994, hundreds were killed in the Catholic church and among the forested hills of the area. A few individuals survived the massacre by stealing out at night to search for food and water, then hiding during the day, under the dead bodies that lay in the church.

Eventually, the bodies at Kibuye's church were buried in a mass grave nearby. Between the end of 1995 and the beginning of 1996, the grave was excavated and the bodies exhumed. The surrounding hills were also searched for bodies. This operation was carried out under the auspices of UNAMIR (United Nations Assistance Mission to Rwanda), with the assistance of Physicians for Human Rights, based in Boston, Massachusetts. Before anything

could be done, the area had to be searched for mines, while the individuals involved in the field work were protected by United Nations military personnel.

Many skeletonized bodies of escapees were retrieved among the hills. The mass grave was exhumed using specialized archeological techniques and the bodies of nearly 500 men, women, and children were recovered.

Each body was autopsied by a forensic pathologist, after which the biological profile (age, sex, stature, and any other notable characteristics) was assessed by the anthropologist. Because entire families had been killed, DNA testing was not carried out. Moreover, positive identification with the aid of dental and medical records was not possible, because such records did not exist. Instead,

the clothing retrieved from the bodies and other personal effects found with them were displayed in the hope that someone would identify them. However, few of the items were recognized. Yet the work done in Rwanda made the world aware of the brutality that had taken place during those 100 days, and the people who had been killed eventually received a dignified burial.

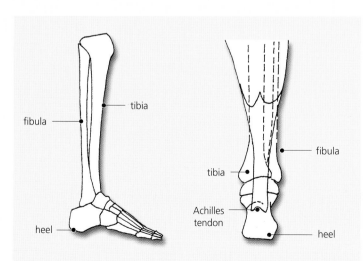

opposite A man holds a panga, an agricultural tool used widely in Rwanda.

top left Victims of the genocide lie decomposing in the streets of Kigali.

top right The clothes of the victims are displayed in the hope of being identified, at Kibuye's Catholic Church.

left Victims were struck with pangas on the achilles tendon, severing it to stop them fleeing.

overleaf Skulls at a genocide memorial church in Rwanda.

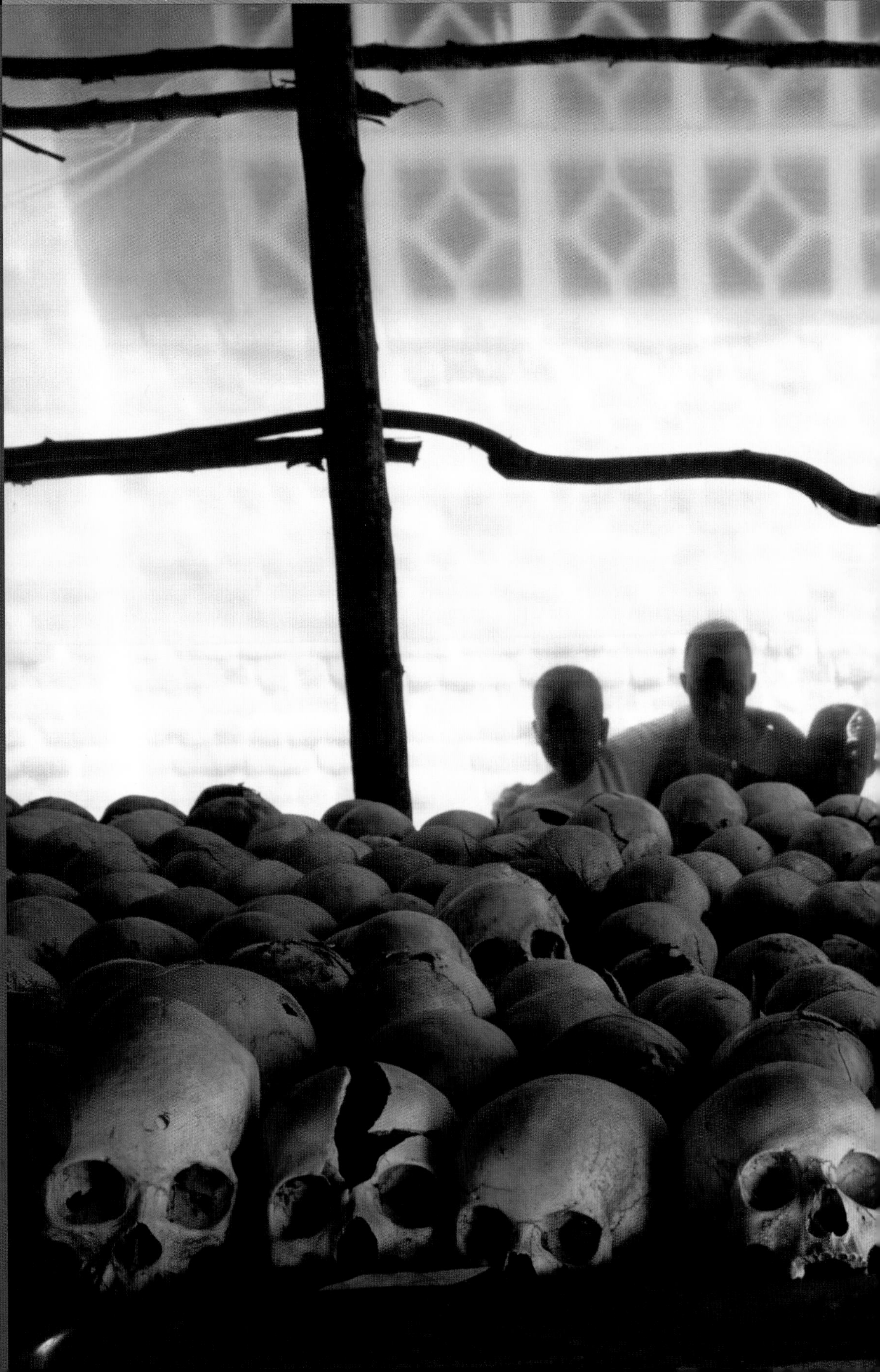

The Massacres

The Central American country of Guatemala has been home to the Mayan people since pre-Columbian times. Although many of their traditions were modified under Spanish influence, they retained their native dress, cooking techniques, and a culture of respect for their elders.

For a large part of its history, Guatemala has remained in the hands of a few elite families, who have exercised great control over economic and political matters. In 1962, the situation deteriorated when the ruling body attempted to retain control of the country by employing a variety of exclusive and racist actions against the population. This marked the beginning of a series of executions, disappearances, massacres, and various other forms of human rights violation.

In the following 34 years of military control, it is estimated that approximately 200,000 people perished—mainly those of Mayan descent—regardless of sex, age, and social status.

One of the many atrocities to have occurred in Guatemala was the Rio Negro Massacre, which bears the name of the area in which it took place, located 155 miles (250 km) north of Guatemala City. In the early 1980s, it was announced that a massive dam would be built at Rio Negro, as part of the Chixoy Hydroelectric Project. Those who lived in the locality were opposed to the creation of the dam, since the land had been their home for generations and was blessed with a good fertile soil. In exchange for relocating, they were to receive poor agricultural land, which would have been disastrous for a community that depended heavily upon farming.

Several massacres took place at Rio Negro, including one in March 1982. The victims were mainly women and children—the men had fled the area in an attempt to escape, believing that their wives and children would be safe. The women were raped and killed and the children were smashed against rocks. Afterward, the men responsible for the act dumped the 177 bodies into a ravine.

It was not until 1993 that the bodies were recovered with the participation of the Guatemalan Forensic Anthropology Team. The task took three months to complete, since the recovery of the bodies required time and care, and some had suffered damage from scavenging.

The bones recovered had suffered traumas from blows to the head, and gunshot and stab wounds. Some fetal bones were found, indicating that pregnant women had been killed. The bodies were given a proper burial, accompanied by Mayan rituals.

In total, about 350 people from Rio Negro died in the various massacres. The dam was built, and the survivors from the community were not compensated adequately. Their culture, not only at Rio Negro, but throughout the Mayan community, suffered as a result—traditional rituals are no longer followed and they are obligated to hide their ethnic identity. But despite seeing their people tortured, raped, abducted, and killed, the Mayans have never given up and continue to survive as an ethnic group, gaining strength from their long and proud history.

opposite A forensic anthropologist prepares a skeletonized body before removing it from a mass grave.

right Dr. Clyde Snow (left) examines the skeletons of victims unearthed from a massacre site in northern Guatemala.

below Mayan Indians take part in a wake combining Roman Catholic and Mayan religious rituals.

The Dirty War

A military government took power in Argentina in 1976, after the presidency of María Estela "Isabel" Martínez de Perón had been toppled. Immediately, the military junta began to take violent action against those considered to be leftwing, subversive, or potential opponents of the new regime. This repression was referred to by the perpetrators as the "Guerra Sucia" (Dirty War). It was typified by kidnappings of civilians who shared a different political view to that of the military regime: intellectuals, students, journalists, and lawyers who would not cooperate with the regime. The most oppressed area was Buenos Aires, between 1976 and 1978.

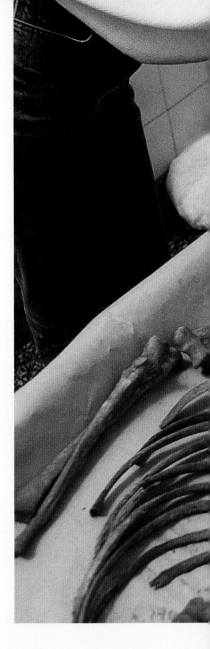

Kidnappings could occur anywhere, from victims' homes to public areas. Once in the junta's grasp, and safely under guard, those seized were transported to one of the 300 clandestine detention centers in the country. There, they were confined and tortured, some enduring years of detention. No one was spared—even children and the elderly were subjected to various types of torture. Some died in the process, others were sent to official prisons, but most were either shot or drugged and taken aboard military aircraft, from which they would be dumped while still alive, over the River Plate, between Argentina and Uruguay. Eventually, the bodies would be washed up on the shores of both countries. Pregnant women were also tortured, and when their delivery time came, the newborn children were taken away to be sold on the black market, handed over to orphanages, or adopted by members of the military.

Most of the bodies were disposed of in mass and individual graves in cemeteries throughout the country, although some individuals were cremated. The bodies that were buried were fingerprinted and autopsied, and a death certificate issued and registered in the cemetery records under "NN" (No Name). Although the names had been withheld, these records were of use later in the location of the remains and their eventual identification.

It is estimated that 10,000 people died in the detention centers, but a lucky few survived and were eventually released. In time, these survivors would assist in the location of the disappeared, by providing relevant information to the authorities.

During the Dirty War, the families of the disappeared never knew the fate of their loved ones. Desperate to find out what had happened to their children and grandchildren, some women began to gather once a week at the Plaza de Mayo in Buenos Aires, to make their views public. Eventually, hundreds of women would congregate, all demanding the whereabouts of the children. They became known as Las Madres de la Plaza de Mayo (Mothers of the Plaza de Mayo) and Las Abuelas de la Plaza de Mayo (Grandmothers of the Plaza de Mayo). Some of the latter had never seen their grandchildren, because the babies had been born at the detention centers. They started to do their own detective work, and were watched closely by the military; in time, some of them disappeared too.

Approximately 500 children were abducted during the rule of the military regime. With the advent of DNA testing during the 1980s, new hope was given to the grandparents of being reunited with their grandchildren. Yet despite the investigations and the use of DNA analysis, only a fraction

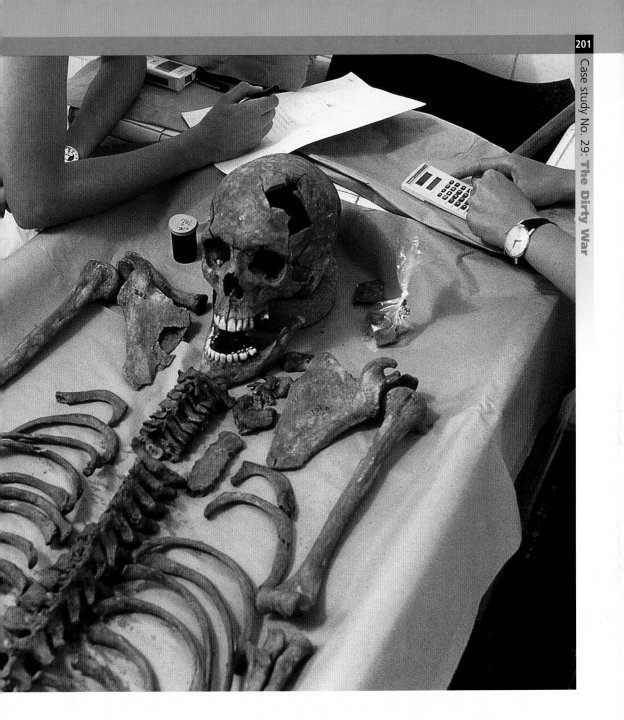

of the children have been found. Nonetheless, the women continue to search, some having taken as long as 10 years to locate their grandchildren.

In 1982, Argentina became involved in a war with the United Kingdom, following the former's invasion of the Falkland Islands. The invaders were ousted from the islands by British forces, and the Argentine military government began to lose support, widespread unrest developing in the country. Under pressure, the government called an election and, after seven years of military oppression, Argentina was on its way to being a democracy, under Raul Alfonsin, who was elected president.

Because executions were carried out throughout the country and a large number of people disappeared, the forensic team's task of locating the bodies proved monumental. The search has continued through the years, aided by the testimony of relatives, friends, and former detainees. Moreover, investigators have had to carry out detective work to find dental and medical records to assist in the positive identification of the bodies they exhume.

The Argentine Forensic Anthropology Team has created a database that helps in the search for and identification of the victims. They have also been responsible for setting up a blood bank, to which surviving relatives have donated blood samples, and from which genetic information is gathered and recorded to be compared with DNA extracted from the bodies that are exhumed.

The team continues to search Argentina for the disappeared, and its expertise is recognized around the world.

As a result, they have assisted in investigations in Ethiopia, Bolivia, and Chile, among a great many other countries.

above One of the mothers of the Plaza de Mayo holding her daughter's picture.

left An Argentinian cemeteries with unidentified graves.

The Death Caravans

Augusto Pinochet came to power in Chile in 1973, after ousting President-elect Salvador Allende. During the first weeks following the coup, the country was kept under martial law, and the new regime began to kidnap, torture, and kill those who were considered foes of the new government, such as labor union members, students, intellectuals, and communists.

As weeks went by, people who had been seized were taken to several detention centers— known as the "death caravans." The national soccer stadium in Santiago became a center for detention. Thousands of people were held there and at other centers throughout the country, such as Villa Grimaldi and Colonia Dignidad, where individuals were routinely tortured. Any place could be turned into a prison camp, as was the case of an old wooden barracks at a military outpost, which did not even have the basic facilities for hygiene. The families of those who disappeared requested a list of the detained, but to no avail.

It is estimated that thousands of people were arrested, tortured, and killed on Pinochet's specific orders. The bodies were either buried in mass graves or dumped from helicopters over the Pacific Ocean. Some of the bodies were washed up on the country's beaches, but many remain on the list of the disappeared.

The killings were not only perpetrated in Chile, but also overseas. The head of Chile's National Intelligence Directorate (DINA), Colonel Contreras, oversaw both the death caravans and "Operation Condor," which aimed to hunt down those who opposed the Pinochet regime. Assassinations were carried out in Italy, Argentina, and the United States. Contreras was given a seven-year prison sentence in 1995 for the killings carried out in the United States.

Many mass graves have been discovered, and the bodies retrieved, since Pinochet's dictatorship came to an end in 1990. Because the condition of some of the remains makes their identification almost impossible by conventional methods, the Argentine Forensic Anthropology Team has helped in the collection of blood samples from the relatives

of those who disappeared. From the available remains, DNA is extracted and compared to the samples. It is expected that more remains will be recovered and identified in the future, but the exact number of those killed during the years of terror in Chile may never be known.

opposite Augusto Pinochet, accused of ordering political killings.

left Forensic experts excavate a former police station, south of Santiago, where several skeletons were unearthed.

below Political prisoners line up in Santiago's Tres Alamos Prison Camp, shortly before their release, as part of a liberation program.

overleaf Relatives of those who "disappeared" during Pinochet's dictatorship stand underneath the Memorial for the Detained and Disappeared in Santiago, Chile.

HA QUEDADO PEGADO A LAS

Spanish Mass Killings

The Spanish Civil War (1936-1939) was brought on by a series of issues including continued economic problems, reduced industrial production, high unemployment, and land laid fallow or moved into governmental control. This gave rise to civil unrest, political divisions, and power shifts. After the murder of right-wing politician José Calvo-Sotelo by leftwing elements, the military, led by Francisco Franco took decisive control. The Civil War started in July 1936.

Following years of economic unrest and dissatisfaction within the working classes, the Spanish Civil War brought turmoil to a nation already divided between factions, mainly left- and rightwing groups. Owing to existing divisions and the war being waged by the military, those considered leftwing, known as Republicans, were brutally persecuted. Individuals were accused without foundation to settle old scores, to gain property and other valuable commodities, or influence within a given region; entire communities and families were divided on political views.

This environment led to situations in which no one knew whom to trust. Hunger was an everyday event and those on the run were forced to starve, being dependent on those willing to risk their lives by supplying staples, or endangering themselves by approaching communities in the hopes of stealing food. Many were found out and summarily executed, regardless of age and sex.

Those who remained in their communities with families, making a living in various activities, were rounded up and either summarily executed or taken to local jails, with families told that they were

right General Francisco Franco lead the fascist troops during the Spanish Civil War, and was dictator of Spain from 1939 to 1975.

required to answer questions and would soon return. But these individuals were later executed and buried in mass graves which were hidden in isolated regions and along roads; families, including their children, remained awaiting their return.

During three years of war, hundreds of thousands perished; this was compounded by the brutal dictatorship that followed led by General Franco. Opponents were persecuted, tortured, imprisoned, and executed, including young individuals.

Today, the Association for the Recuperation of Historic Memory organizes, through family appeals, the search, location, and recovery of those who disappeared over a 39-year span. This work is conducted by members, mostly volunteers, from many walks of

right Portrait of José Calvo-Sotelo whose murder in 1936 triggered the Spanish Civil War.

below The sole of a boot and the skeletal remains of a person killed during General Franco's dictatorship, in the San Rafael mass grave in Málaga.

life, including those with missing relatives. Forensic anthropologists also volunteer to assist in the recovery of remains from graves, and briefly assess the age and sex of the victims.

Work in the field can be challenging, as much time has lapsed, and memories are fading on the part of witnesses who were young at the time; many days may be spent in searches before succeeding. Usually, a mechanical digger is utilized to extract the soil and fill, as a considerable amount has accumulated over the years. Once remains or artifacts are noted, archeological techniques are applied by careful use of hand tools. Despite the many years that have past, in normal circumstances the bone tissue is in very good condition.

Within the laboratory, a profile of each set of remains (age, sex, stature, and individual characteristics) is compiled, and the results compared with information gathered. Sometimes a profile may not fit the description provided of those within the grave. Further investigations may be required, which delay the identification process. This is a serious issue, as the work is a race against time; family members who have been searching for decades are often of an advanced age. Trauma is also assessed, which normally consists of a single or multiple gunshot wounds to the head.

Once properly identified, the remains are returned to the respective families, upon which a ceremony and burial takes place, providing a final and proper rest.

above An archeologist exhumes human remains at the San Rafael mass grave in Málaga where over 3,000 bodies were located, including women and children.

left A mechanical digger is used to excavate a mass grave. The depth of some sites is remarkable as they fill up with soil and other materials over the years.

The Katyn Massacre

The Katyn Massacre, also referred to as the Katyn Forest Massacre, took place during World War II, near Smolensk, within Soviet territory. The victims were mainly officers and enlisted men of the Polish military, but also included members of the Polish intellectual community and the clergy, totaling approximately 15,000 individuals. Their disappearance caused much concern in Poland; blame was imparted mutually between the Germans and Soviets.

below Thousands of bodies of the Polish military prisoners exhumed in 1943 at Katyn Forest.

During World War II (1939-1945), mutual interests between the German and Soviet governments led to the invasion of Poland in 1939. The country was heavily assaulted by the German Blitzkrieg, weakening its infrastructure and claiming many casualties. Poland buckled and prisoners were taken by the Soviets, including civilians; over a million died due to overwork, disease, and starvation.

Over the months, Soviet and German relations froze, with the Soviets being drawn to the side of the Allies, culminating in an agreement with Poland to join forces and fight Germany. Prisoners held at many camps were released, though thousands were unaccounted for. During the turmoil of War World II, this was a problematic issue to investigate, although strong efforts were made through diplomatic channels. The Soviet Union insisted that they had no knowledge of the matter.

In 1941, Germany invaded the Soviet Union, using in part Polish labor forces. While in the Katyn area, workers discovered bodies in Polish military uniforms. The local population were hesitant to talk, although they had witnessed first-hand the transport of the victims via trains and trucks, and also heard gun fire. The Germans became aware of this, and were eager to settle the issue as they were implicated as being responsible.

The Polish authorities contacted the International Red Cross, and it was agreed to investigate the site, providing that all concerned approved the intervention; however, The Soviet Union strongly opposed such an action. The German Red Cross though offered

to pursue the investigation in co-operation with the Polish Red Cross and non-German forensic medical personnel. In early 1943, the international intervention began. Eight mass graves were located within the woods at the Hill of Goats. Over 4,000 bodies were exhumed, the largest grave containing over 2,000 people. The

principal role of the medical professionals was to establish the cause of death, identify the victims, and determine when the killings had occurred.

The exhumations revealed that the bodies were carefully laid out in the graves, several rows deep; the condition of the bodies varied, with some still retaining decomposing

tissue, whereas others presented mummification. Fractures and bayonet wounds were observed. There were also close-range entrance gunshot wounds to the back of the head with the exit wound at the forehead level. Many still possessed personal documents, including diaries and letters, which aided in identifying specific individuals and dating the time of the massacre accurately.

By today's standards, the postmortem examinations in the field seem basic, and lacking protocols; the work was accomplished in two days, with few individuals being examined. Today, by contrast, human rights investigations involve mobile units manned with international personnel who will be available for the required duration.

The investigations resulted in two major findings: the Massacre had to have occurred in 1940, and the ammunition was of German manufacture. The irony was that the Germans had not invaded the region until 1941. Furthermore, the ammunition had been sold to the Red Army years earlier.

Several years after the fact, the Soviet Union finally accepted culpability. Prisoners had been

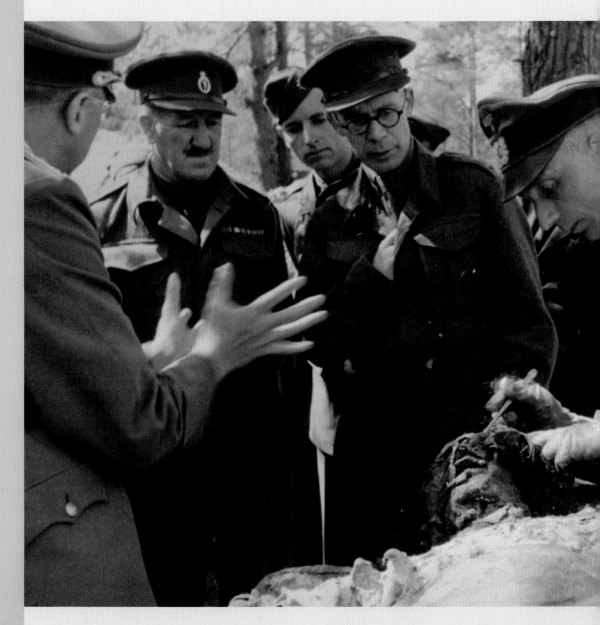

detained in three camps: Kozielsk and Ostashkow, both within Soviet territory, and Starobielsk, which was within Soviet control at the time.

During the 70th anniversary of the Katyn Massacre, the Polish prime minister attended a ceremony in Russia—an unprecedented move given the historically strained relationship between the countries.

above Katyn Forest, Russia. Mass grave of Polish soldiers being investigated by the German military and Red Cross personnel.

left Autopsies were conducted on site at Katyn.

Conclusion

The preceding chapters demonstrate the diverse manner in which forensic anthropologists can, and have, assisted in the identification of the victims of airplane and railroad accidents, terrorist acts, murders, and fires, among a variety of often bizarre events resulting in death. Their specialized knowledge of human osteology is invaluable, making it possible for investigators to close cases that would otherwise have remained unsolved.

Although forensic anthropology began in earnest during the late 1800s, the techniques that were developed then, and continue to be used today, have grown in scope and effectiveness. Forensic anthropologists are constantly extending their knowledge of the human skeleton, and the inherent, and often frustrating, variability that it presents. This continual process has led to many new and innovative investigative techniques that play an important role in the correct identification of human remains.

Forensic anthropology has rightfully earned a valued place within the framework of the forensic sciences and currently is regarded as an integral element of many crime investigations. It is also employed increasingly in the aftermath of mass disasters and other situations in which the accurate identification of human remains is necessary. Inevitably, forensic anthropology forms part of a multidisciplinary investigative approach in which many aspects of the forensic field, such as DNA analysis, forensic entomology, and archeology, are utilized to great effect.

On a personal level, forensic anthropologists achieve gratification in being able to assist in identifying accurately the remains of individuals whose lives have been cut short. More importantly, however, their work can provide some peace of mind for victims' loved ones, who may be scarred and traumatized by their loss. The participation of forensic anthropologists in human rights cases has often served as a catalyst for the healing process to begin on both a personal and social level, offering societies and cultures the opportunity to flourish once again.

Right Forensic anthropologists examine a decomposed body while the assistant on the left records relevant information.

Bibliography

Angyal, M., and Derczy, K., *Personal Identification on the Basis of Antemortem and Postmortem Radiographs*, Journal of Forensic Sciences, JFSCA, Vol. 43, No. 5, September 1998, pp. 1089–1093.

Asociación para la Recuperación de la Memoria Histórica (ARMH). www.memoriahistorica.org.es/joomla

BBC News, http://news.bbc.co.uk/1/hi/magazine/7348164.stm

Bennett, J.L., and Rockhold, L.A., *Use of an Alternate Light Source for Tattoo Recognition in the Extended Postmortem Interval*, Journal of Forensic Sciences, JFSCA, Vol. 44, No. 1, January 1999, pp. 182–184.

Bennett, K.A., *Victim Selection in the Jeffrey Dahmer Slayings: An Example of Repetition in the Paraphilias?*, Journal of Forensic Sciences, JFSCA, Vol. 38, No. 5, September 1993, pp. 1227–1232.

Bouchrika, I., et al., *On Using Gait in Forensic Biometrics*, Journal of Forensic Sciences, JFSCA, Vol. 56, No. 4, July 2011, pp. 882–889.

Byers, S., *Introduction to Forensic Anthropology* (3rd ed.), London, Pearson, 2008.

Bugliosi, V., *And The Sea Will Tell*, New York, Ballantine Publishing Group, 1991.

Cave, M., *The Shadow of Doubt*, Historic New Orleans Collection Quarterly, Vol. 19, No. 4, December 2001.

Cope, D., and Dupras, T., *The Effects of Household Corrosive Chemicals on Human Dentition*, Journal of Forensic Sciences, JFSCA, Vol. 54, No. 6, November 2009, pp. 1238–1246.

Crime library, Robert Pickton: The Vancouver Missing Women. www.trutv.com/library/crime/serial_killers/predators/robert_pickton/1.html

Davis, J.L., et al., *Ground Penetrating Radar Surveys to Locate 1918 Spanish Flu Victims in Permafrost*, Journal of Forensic Sciences, JFSCA, Vol. 45, No. 1, January 2000, pp. 68–76.

Delattere, V.F., *Burned Beyond Recognition: Systematic Approach to the Dental Identification of Charred Human Remains*, Journal of Forensic Sciences, JFSCA, Vol. 45, No. 3, May 2000, pp. 589–596.

Dupras, T., et al., *Forensic Recovery of Human Remains: Archaeological Approaches*, Boca Raton, CRC Press, 2012.

Fairgrieve, S.I. (ed.), *Forensic Osteological Analysis: A Book of Case Studies*, Illinois, Charles C. Thomas Publisher, 1999.

FBI. The Federal Bureau of Investigation, Seattle Division www.fbi.gov/seattle/about-us/history-1/history

Ferllini, R., *Rwanda: Political Conflict and Genocide*, Journal on Rehabilitation of Torture Victims and Prevention of Torture, Vol. 7, No. 3, 1997.

Ferllini, R., *Forensic Archaeology and Human Rights Violations*, Springfield, Charles C. Thomas, 2007.

Ferllini, R., *Experiencias en Antropología Forense: Perspectivas de una Voluntaria Extranjera*, Boletin Galego de Medicina Legal e Forense 18, Enero, 2012.

Fitzgibbon, L., *Katyn: A Crime Without Parallel*, London, Tom Stacey, 1971.

Galloway, A. (ed.), *Broken Bones: Anthropological Analysis of Blunt Force Trauma*, Illinois, Charles C. Thomas, 1999.

Haglund, W., *The Use of Hydrogen Peroxide to Visualize Tattos Obscured by Decomposition and Mummification*, Journal of Forensic Sciences, JFSCA, Vol. 38, No. 1, January 1993, pp. 147–150.

Haglund, W., and Reay, D.T., *Problems of Recovering Partial Human Remains at Different Times: Concerns for Death Investigators*, Journal of Forensic Sciences, JFSCA, Vol. 38, No. 1, January 1993, pp. 69–80.

Haglund, W., and Sorg, M.H. (eds.), *Forensic Taphonomy: The Postmortem Fate of Human Remains*, New York, CRC Press, 1997.

Hartnett, K., et al., *The Effects of Corrosive Substances on Human Bone, Teeth, Hair, Nails, and Soft Tissue*, Journal of Forensic Sciences, JFSCA, Vol. 56, No. 4, July 2011, pp. 954–959.

Humphrey, J., and Hutchinson, D., *Macroscopic Characteristics of Hacking Trauma*, Journal of Forensic Sciences, JFSCA, Vol. 46, No. 2, March 2001, 228–233.

Ishii, M., et al., *Application of Superimposition-Based Personal Identification Using Skull Computed Tomography Images*, Journal of Forensic Sciences, JFSCA, Vol.56, No.4, July 2011, pp. 960–966.

Jones, S., *Wicked London*, Nottingham, Wicked Publications, 1999.

Joyce, C., and Stover, E., *Witness from the Grave: The Stories Bones Tell*, New York, Ballantine Books, 1992.

Kahana, T., et al., *Suicidal Terrorist Bombing in Israel – Identification of Human Remains*, Journal of Forensic Sciences, JFSCA, Vol. 42, No. 2, March 1997, pp. 260–264.

Kahana, T., et al., *Marine Taphonomy: Adipocere Formation in a Series of Bodies Recovered from a Single Shipwreck*, Journal of Forensic Sciences, JFSCA, Vol. 44, No. 5, September 1999, pp. 897–901.

Kennedy, K., *The Wrong Urn: Commingling of Cremains in Mortuary Practices*, Journal of Forensic Sciences, JFSCA, Vol. 41, No. 4, July 1996, pp. 689–692.

Larsen, P., et al., *Gait Analysis in Forensic Medicine*, Journal of Forensic Sciences, JFSCA, Vol. 53, No. 5, September 2008, pp.1149–1153.

Larsen P., et al., *Variability of Bodily Measures of Normally Dressed People using Photo Modeler® Pro 5*, Journal of Forensic Sciences, JFSCA, Vol. 53, No. 6, November 2008, pp. 1393–1399.

Lee, W., et al., *An Accuracy Assessment of Forensic Computerized Facial Reconstruction Employing Cone-Beam Computed Tomography from Live Subjects*, Journal of Forensic Sciences, Vol. 57, No. 2, March 2012, pp. 318–327.

Leonetti, G., et al., *Evidence of Pin Implantation as a Means of Verifying Death During the Great Plague of Marseilles (1722)*, Journal of Forensic Sciences, JFSCA, Vol. 42, No. 4, July 1997, pp. 744–748.

Levinson, J,and Granot, H., *Transportation Disaster Response Handbook*, New York, Academic Press, 2002.

Lynnerup N., and Vedel, J., *Person Identification by Gait Analysis and Photogrammetry*, Journal of Forensic Sciences, JFSCA, Vol. 50, No. 1, January 2005, pp. 112–118.

Lynnerup. N., et al., Identification by Facial Recognition, Gait Analysis and Photogrammetry: The Anna Lindh Murder, in Brickley, M., Ferllini, R, (Eds.), *Forensic Anthropology: Case Studies from Europe*, Springfield, Charles C. Thomas, 2007, pp.232–244.

McQueen, K., How Serial Killer Robert Pickton Slipped Away: New Revelations Show Why He Was Able to Prey with Such Impunity, August 23rd, 2010, www.missingpeople.net/how_serial_killer_robert_pickton.htm

Maples, W., and Browning, M., *Dead Men do Tell Tales: The Strange and Fascinating Cases of a Forensic Anthropologist*, (2nd ed.), London, Arrow Books, 1998.

Mendoza, A., *Killers on the Loose: Unsolved Cases of Serial Murder*, London, Virgin, 2000.

Min, J.-X., and Jia, M.-Z., *Correlation of Trauma and Cause of Death to Accident Reconstruction: A Case of a Flight Accident Report*, Journal of Forensic Sciences, JFSCA, Vol. 37, No. 2, March 1992, pp. 585–589.

NecroSearch International. www.necrosearch.com/ Accessed March 9th, 2012

Nolte, K., et al., *Insect Larvae Used to Detect Cocaine Poisoning in a Decomposed Body*, Journal of Forensic Sciences, JFSCA, Vol. 37, No. 4, July 1992, pp. 1179–1185.

Otner, D.J., and Putschar, W.G.J., *Identification of Pathological Conditions in Human Skeletal Remains*, Washington, Smithsonian Institution Press, 1985.

Owsley, D., *Identification of the Fragmentary, Burned Remains of Two U.S. Journalists Seven Years Ago After Their Disappearance in Guatemala*, Journal of Forensic Sciences, JFSCA, Vol. 38, No. 6, November 1993, pp.1372–1382.

Owsley, D.W., et al., *Positive Identification in a Case of Intentional Extreme Fragmentation*, Journal of Forensic Sciences, JFSCA, Vol. 38, No. 4, July 1993, pp. 985–996.

Owsley, D.W., et al., *The Role of Forensic Anthropology in the Recovery Analysis of Branch Davidian Compound Victims: Techniques of Analysis*, Journal of Forensic Sciences, JFSCA, Vol. 40, No. 3, May 1995, pp. 341–348.

Patel, F., *Artefact in Forensic Medicine: Postmortem Rodent Activity*, Journal of Forensic Sciences, JFSCA, Vol. 39, No. 1, January 1994, pp. 257–260.

Pfeiffer, S., et al., *The Natural Decomposition of Adipocere*, Journal of Forensic Sciences, JFSCA, Vol. 43, No. 2, March 1998, pp. 368–370.

Physicians for Human Rights (PHR). http://physiciansforhumanrights.org/issues/mass-atrocities/afghanistan-transitional-justice

Pickering, T., *Carnivore Voiding: A Taphonomic Process with the Potential for the Decomposition of Forensic Evidence*, Journal of Forensic Sciences, JFSCA, Vol. 46, No. 2, March 2001, pp. 406–411.

Pollanen, M.S., and Chiasson, D.A., *Fracture of the Hyoid Bone in Strangulation: Comparison of Fractured and Unfractured Hyoids from Victims of Strangulation*, Journal of Forensic Sciences, JFSCA, Vol. 41, No. 1, January 1996, pp. 110–113.

Preston, P., *The Spanish Civil War. Reaction, Revolution, Revenge*, London, Harper Perennial, 2006.

Prunier, G., *The Rwanda Crisis: History of a Genocide*, Kampala, Fountain Publishers, 1995.

Pye, K, Croft, D., (eds.), *Forensic Geoscience: Principles, Techniques and Applications*, London, Geological Society, 2004.

Ramstrand, N., et al., *Relative Effects of Posture and Activity on Human Height Estimation from Surveillance Footage*, Forensic Science International, Vol. 212, No. 1-3, October 2011, pp. 27–31.

Rutty, G.M. et al., *The Role of Mobile Computed Tomography in Mass Fatality Incidents*, Journal of Forensic Sciences, Vol. 52, No. 6, November 2007, pp.1343–1349.

Sakuma, A.,et al., *Application of Postmortem 3D-CT Facial Reconstruction for Personal Identification*, Journal of Forensic Sciences, JFSCA, Vol. 55, No. 6, November 2010, pp. 1624–1629, 2010.

Scott, A., et al., *Anthropological and Radiographic Comparison of Antemortem Surgical Records for Identification of Skeletal Remains*, Journal of Forensic Sciences, JFSCA, Vol. 55, No.1, January 2010, pp. 241–244.

Seabrook, J., *In the Rubble: The Unknown*, The New Yorker, posted 9-24-2001

Sharkey, J., *Above Suspicion*, New York, St Martin's Press, 1994.

Stewart, T.D., *Essentials of Forensic Anthropology*, Springfield, Charles C. Thomas, 1989.

The Vancouver Sun, Robert Pickton on trail, www2.canada.com/vancouversun/features/pickton/archive.html

Ubelaker, D.H., *The Remains of Dr. Carl Austin Weiss: Anthropological Analysis*, Journal of Forensic Sciences, JFSCA, Vol. 41, No. 1, January 1996, pp. 60–79.

Ubelaker, D., and O'Donnell, G., *Computer-Assisted Facial Reproduction*, Journal of Forensic Sciences, JFSCA, Vol. 37, No. 1, January 1992, pp. 155–162.

Ubelaker, D.H., and Scammell, H., *Bones: A Forensic Detective's Casebook*, New York, M. Evans, 1992.

Ubelaker, D., et al., *Computer-Assisted Photographic Superimposition*, Journal of Forensic Sciences, JFSCA, Vol. 37, No. 3, May 1992, pp. 750–762.

Ubelaker, D.H., et al., *The Role of Forensic Anthropology in the Recovery and Analysis of Branch Davidian Compound Victims: Recovery, Procedure and Characteristics of the Victims,*

Journal of Forensic Sciences, JFSCA, Vol. 40, No. 3, May 1995, pp. 335–340.

Ubelaker, D., Soren, B. (eds.), *Handbook of Forensic Archaeology and Anthropology*, Walnut Creek, Left Coast, 2009.

Warren, M., et al., *Use of Radiographic Atlases in a Mass Fatality*, Journal of Forensic Sciences, JFSCA, Vol. 45, No. 2, March 2000, pp. 467–470.

Wecht, C., *Grave Secrets*, London, Penguin, 1998.

Whyte, K., "Hinton's head-on horror," Albert Report news magazine, February 17, 1986.

Wilkes, D.E. *Who Killed the Kingfish?* The Athens Observer, p. 8A, September 12, 1985.

Zawodny, J.K, *Death in the Forest: The Story of the Katyn Forest Massacre*, Notre Dame, Notre Dame University Press, 1971.

Glossary

Adipose tissue the fat tissue in the body.

Antemortem before death.

Anthropometry the study of the measurements of the human body by using special calipers.

Autopsy the examination of the tissues and organs by a forensic pathologist to determine the cause of death.

Celts a cultural group that originated in Alpine Europe and later spread to the Iberian Peninsula. They were known for their ironwork and farming. At the beginning of the first century BC, the Celts were defeated by Germanic tribes as well as by the Roman Empire, forcing them to retreat to areas of Britain, Ireland, and Northern France.

Charred burned only partially.

Clandestine grave a grave that has been made in secrecy.

Computer Tomography Scan (CT Scan) a special type of X-ray machine which uses a series of beams simultaneously from different directions, allowing cross section views of the body. The technology allows to view images in 2D and 3D.

Concentration camp a prison camp for civilians arrested during a war. In Hitler's Nazi regime in Germany, they were known as extermination camps, since Jews were killed there in great numbers.

Cremation disposal of a body by burning.

Datum a fixed point of reference from which archeological measurements are taken from.

Disappeared individuals who have been abducted by governmental forces.

DNA Deoxyribonucleic acid, which carries the genetic blueprint of each individual; it is used to identify human remains by comparison with the DNA of a close relative.

DVI disaster victim identification

Facial reconstruction the reconstruction of the facial bones following damage caused by trauma.

Facial reproduction the reproduction of facial characteristics using a variety of methods.

Forensic an investigation of a crime using scientific means, also the application of scientific knowledge to legal matters.

Forensic anthropology the field of anthropology that deals with the identification of human remains by examining the bones.

Forensic archeology the application of archeological techniques in the forensic field to carry out an exhumation.

Forensic entomology the study of insects in relation to a crime scene in an attempt to estimate the time since death, or determine whether a body has been moved from the place of the crime.

Forensic odontology a branch of dentistry that deals with the identification of human bodies by examination of the dental remains.

Forensic pathology a branch of medicine that deals with the examination of dead bodies' soft tissues to determine the cause of death.

Furnace a structure in which a fuel is used to produce heat.

Genocide the systematic destruction of a group of people because of their national, religious, ethnic, or political affiliation.

Holocaust the extermination of European Jews by the German Nazi regime under Adolf Hitler during the 1930s and 1940s.

Hyoid bone a bone situated at the base of the tongue, which may break in cases of strangulation.

Incineration burned to ashes.

Junta the military rulers of a country, usually taking power after a coup.

Ligament strong tissue that connects bone with bone at the joints providing flexibility.

Mass disaster an unforeseen event that claims many lives.

Mass grave a grave that contains two or more bodies.

Mass murder the killing of many people by one individual.

Maya a native American group found today in the Mexican Yucatan Peninsula, Guatemala, Honduras, and Belize.

Missing individuals abducted by nongovernmental entities.

Osteology the study of bones.

Postmortem after death; often used to mean autopsy.

Prognathism the projection of the jaw in relation to the upper part of the face.

Saponification when the fat tissue in the body turns into a whitish waxy

substance after being exposed to moisture in an airless environment—for example, submerged under water.

Sharp-force trauma force exerted over a narrow surface.

Sinus a small cavity in the body—for example, the paranasal sinuses, which are connected to the nose by internal passages; when bacteria enters, they become inflamed and cause discomfort, a condition known as sinusitis.

Skeletonization when the body is reduced to bones, with no soft tissues remaining.

SS German Nazi military formation established in 1925, involved in the Holocaust.

Taphonomy the study of the events that can alter human remains, such as scavenging by animals and movement by torrential rain.

Tendon strong connective tissue that joins muscle and bone.

Total station electronic equipment used in surveying.

Trauma an injury or wound inflicted upon the body.

Triage a set of priorities based on the medical attention needed by survivors of a mass disaster.

Zeppelin a cigar-shaped airship built by the Germans in the early part of the 20th century; developed originally for military use, zeppelins were employed subsequently for long-distance commercial flights, including transatlantic journeys. Blunt force trauma - exerted by low velocity implement over a large surface.

Index

Acknowledgments

I am grateful to everyone who, in some way or another, contributed to the realization of this book. However, I would particularly like to extend my sincere thanks to the following people:

Dr. Corinne Duhig for her encouragement and her contributions of information for the text; Mark Goode for his illustrations and input concerning the content of the manuscript; Ivannia Barahona for her constant encouragement, also Theodosina Mena; Nancy Jackson, M.A. Colleen Colbert, Dr. Kurt Nolte, and Ian Jennings, all of whom were most helpful in answering my inquiries; Toria Leitch, who helped with the original formulation of the idea; Helen Stallion, for the extensive picture research; and Corinne Masciocchi for bringing the work to its finished form.

Roxana Ferllini

Picture credits

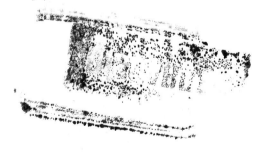